Cyril Mann 1911-1980

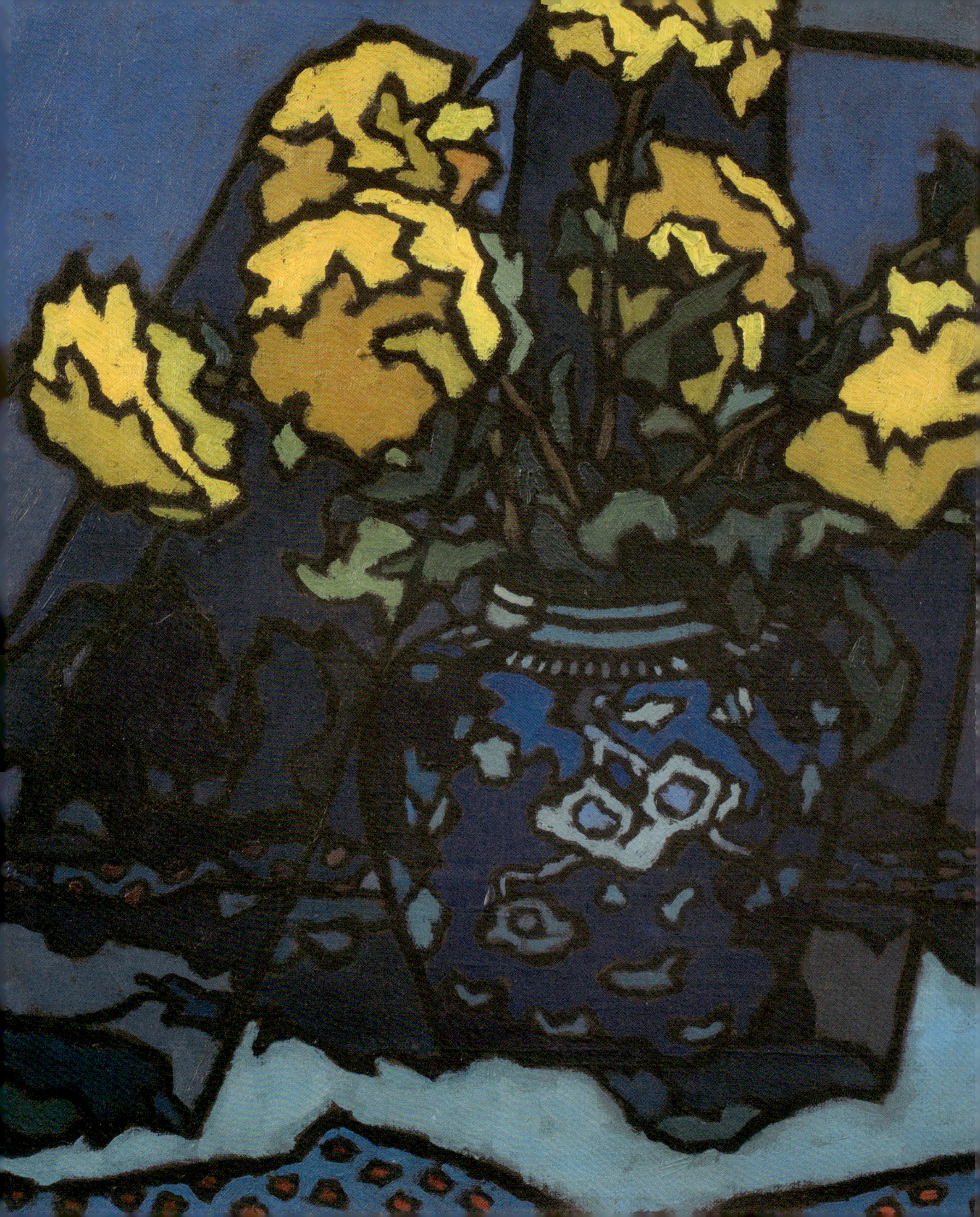

CYRIL MANN

The Solid Shadow Paintings

PIANO
NOBILE

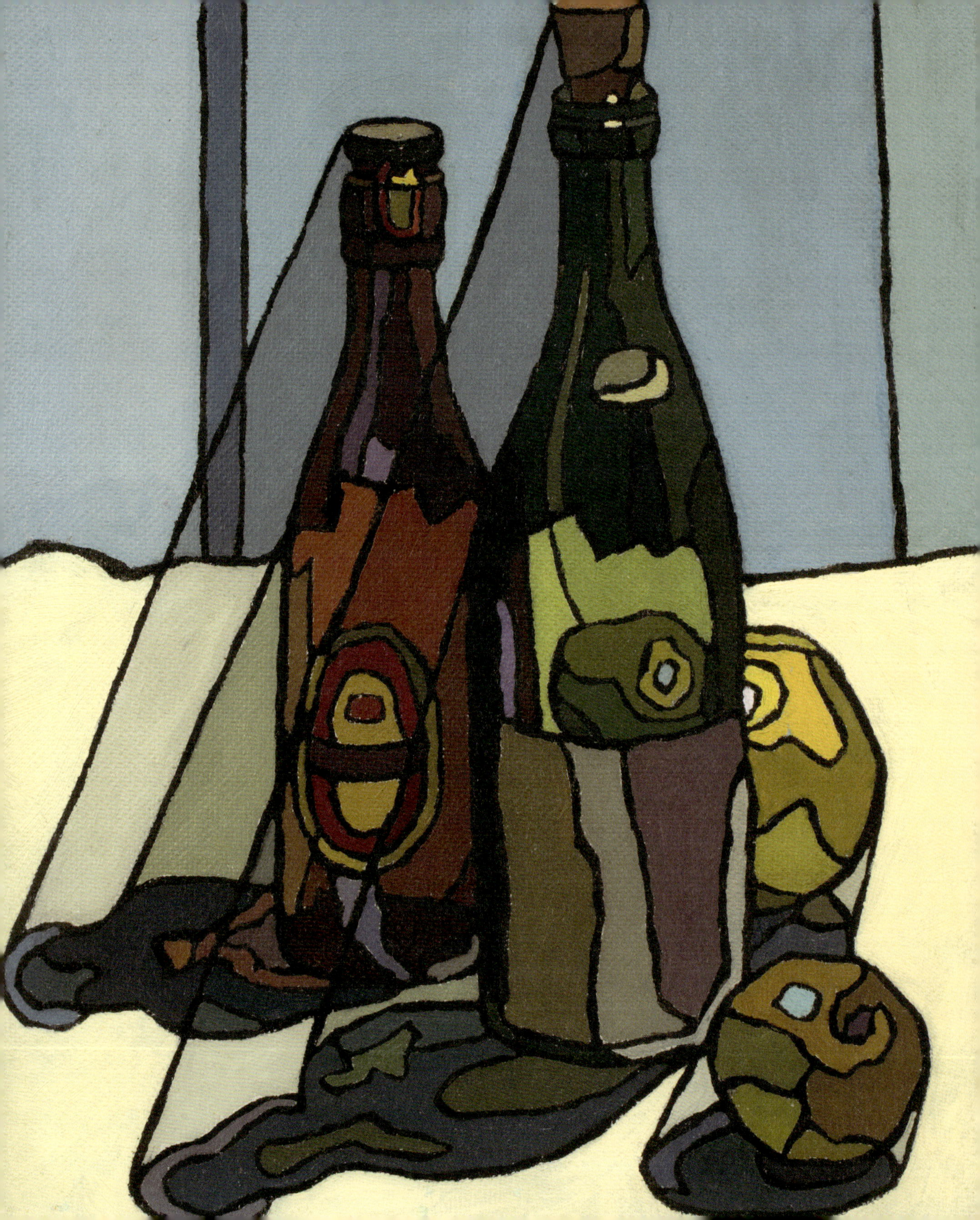

Contents

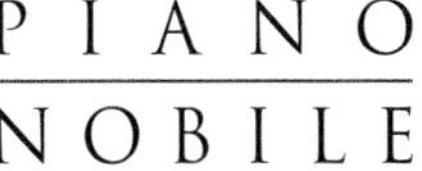

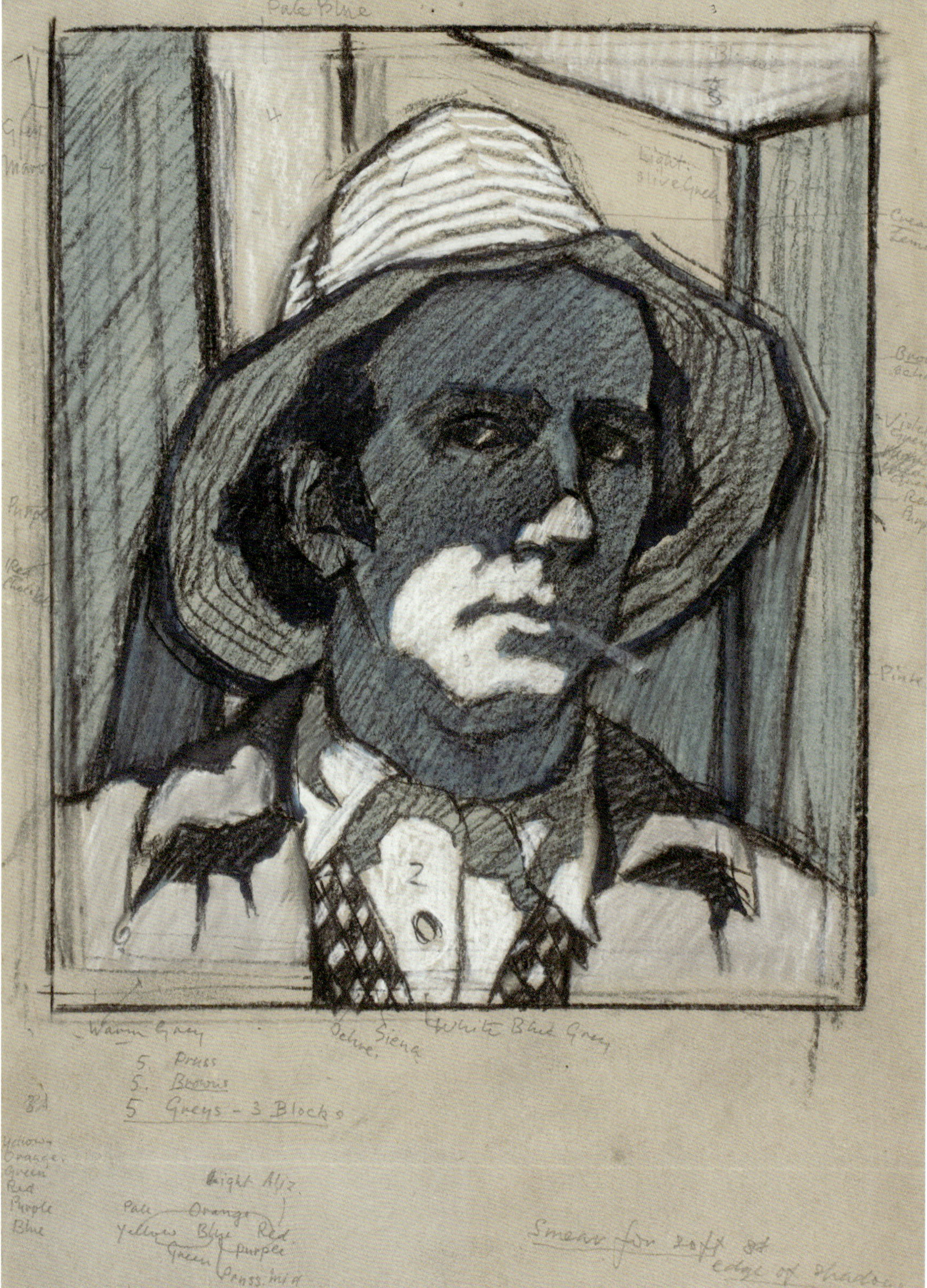
Pale Blue
Light olive Green
Warm Grey
Ochre
Siena
White Blue Grey
5. Pruss
5. Browns
5 Greys - 3 Blocks
Yellow
Orange
Green
Red
Purple
Blue
Light Aliz
Pale Orange
Yellow Blue Red
purple
Green
Pruss. mid
Smear for soft 8t
edge of shadow

Cyril Mann: The Solid Shadow Paintings

In the early fifties, the painter Cyril Mann developed a visual style defined by its hard-edged and stylised shadows. Where previously he had explored the effects of natural light, for a brief period between 1951 and 1957 he experimented instead with the effects of shadow. In the areas of his pictures where light doesn't fall, he created boldly outlined, densely painted surfaces. As such, these works came to be known as the solid shadow paintings.

In the early nineteen-fifties, the local council rehoused Mann to an apartment at 23 Paul Street, near Old Street. The apartment was above a gold bullion broker and there were bars on the windows for insurance purposes. No natural light penetrated into the space. In response to this new situation, Mann flicked the light switch and started working under an artificial glow. With these changed conditions, he observed something that he had previously ignored – the line, usually invisible, which joins an object to the shadow it casts. Though one usually thinks of shadow as a flat dark silhouette, Mann's solid shadow work shows that shadow extends in space, filling the area between an object and the darkened surface behind it.

Though wholly unremarked in histories of the period, these works are notable in the trajectory of twentieth-century British painting. They are marked out by analogy to other distinguished, better studied artists. This shared pictorial style is defined by its stylised manner of boldly outlining shadows and contours. A similar painterly idiom was developed earlier in the century by the Camden Town painters, specifically Robert Bevan and Charles Ginner. In Ginner's *Victoria Embankment Gardens* (1912, Tate Collection) (fig. 2), for example, the crest of each cloud has been delineated with flamboyant, semi-naturalistic colours, and the modelling treated in bold, ungraded tones. There is an evident visual continuity here with Mann's work forty years later.

Fig. 1
Cyril Mann (1911 - 1980)
Self-Portrait, c. 1957

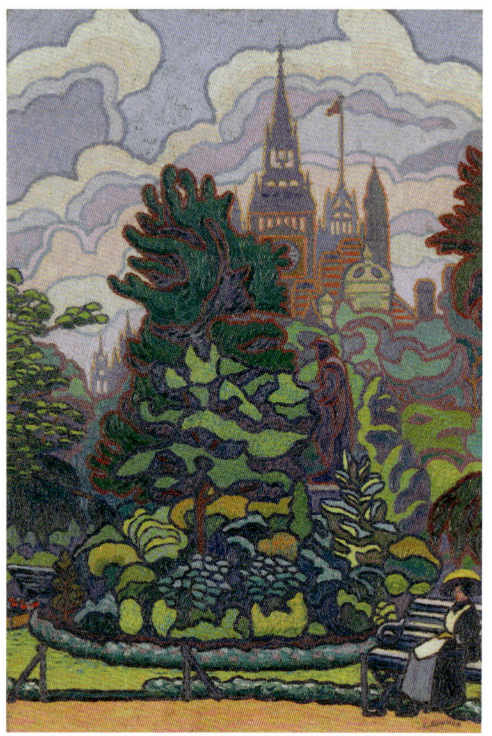

Fig. 2
Charles Ginner (1878 – 1952)
Victoria Embankment Gardens, 1912

Mann's solid shadow paintings were also prescient. They channel a particular kind of pictorial creativity that was not given full expression until the ascendancy of Pop Art. His pictorial schema demonstrates a robust formalism while retaining a representational format which is uncompromised by his exaggerations of colour and line. This accommodation was not arrived at in the wider culture of British painting until the work of Patrick Caulfield in the early nineteen-sixties. Foreshadowing a rich seam of transatlantic artistic activity, including the work of Patrick Caulfield, Michael Craig-Martin, Julian Opie and John Wesley, Mann's bright and carefully delineated paintings are a notable addition to British painting of the post-war period. Indeed, Craig-Martin's much later cycle of lightbulb works, created in 2015 in collaboration with the Serpentine Galleries, might be regarded as a belated corollary to Mann's lightbulb-lit still lifes.

Mann's artistic project was not straightforwardly *avant garde*, however. Though he strove to defy at once his contemporaries and most of his forebears, he also sought out a few select precedents from art history's canon with which to engage. Referring to the Royal Academy, where Mann studied as a student, the critic Mark Hudson has written that he 'excoriated its conventional academicism as much as he did the international avant garde – regarding himself as a genuine, one-man vanguard'.[1] Something of this is communicated by the stylistic singularity of the solid shadow works. With regard to precedents, Cyril's widow, Renske Mann, has described how he engaged in an ongoing discussion with Paul Cézanne, Vincent Van Gogh and Michelangelo (or as he referred to them, Daddy Cézanne, Ol' Van Gogh and Ol' Mike).[2] Often talking aloud to them late into the night, these discussions bore fruit in his paintings. Cézanne pioneered the overt decomposition of a subject, breaking the surface of his picture into clearly delineated segments. In contrast, Van Gogh emphasised the sensuous handling of paint. Michelangelo, in turn, was primarily concerned with the substance of things, their mass and physical presence. All of these aspects, these eclectic artistic interests, inform Mann's solid shadow work. Though they sit uneasily beside contemporary works of their period then, these still lifes are not altogether isolated within a longer history of art.

The bright, hard-edged style of these works has its origin in rigorous preparatory draughtsmanship. The graphic simplicity of Mann's work, as with that of Caulfield, Craig-Martin and the like, owes its clarity to this concealed stage of creativity in which the outlines of a figure or an object are fixed upon, and subsequently reduced to the minimum of outlines necessary to represent the subject in question. Once the outlines are fixed they are simplified, the details of the subject are suppressed, and the colours exaggerated. In keeping with the later work of Opie and Wesley (fig. 5), for example, Mann's solid shadow paintings depend on a comparable process of stylisation for their vital, graphic aesthetic.

His preparatory drawings from this period show how meticulously he composed his still-life subjects. An undated drawing of an apple (fig. 3), for example, is annotated with colour notes. Each segment of the apple's

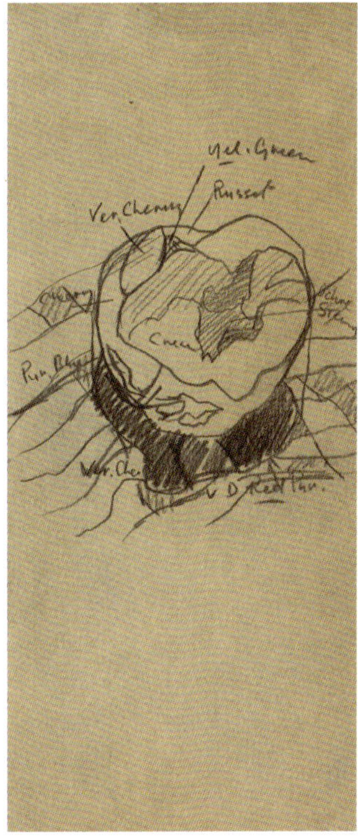

Fig. 3
Cyril Mann (1911 – 1980)
Drawing of an Apple with Colour Notes, c. 1955

surface has a different shade attached – yellow green, russet, purple blue, green, 'V D Red' ('very deep', presumably). Another sheet (cat. 11) shows how Mann addressed the same subject, an apple placed on a bundle of rags, using a mixture of different modelling techniques. Having set down the outlines of the group at the centre of the sheet, he proceeded to repeat it four times at the corner of the sheet. In each rendition, the tonal values are the same – there is light falling on the top of the apple, where there is a small highlight, with deep shadow on the lower front edge of the fruit. Yet in each rendition, a different schema has been used to represent the varying gradations of shadow. In one drawing, Mann has used coarse hatching with a thick pencil, while in another, he has used watercolour to block out segments in subtly varying hues. These preparatory works suggest considerable dexterity of draughtsmanship.

The contours of Mann's preparatory drawings were not just compositionally significant. They also served as an apparatus by which to represent light. Much as Ben Nicholson's contemporary line drawings from the nineteen-fifties accentuate outlines, making them dance and interweave, so too with Mann's solid shadow paintings. The key difference is that Mann's work introduced this new component, a counterpoint of light and shadow, with solid shards of falling light playing around the equally delineated objects themselves.

His representation of light under bare lightbulbs also led him to innovate with stronger, often non-naturalistic colour. As John Russell Taylor has noted, 'Cyril later maintained that his 'solid shadow' phase was important because it made him use strong, bold colours for the first time, and because it compelled him to design his pictures more carefully than ever before'.[3] In a work like *Dahlias in Blue Vase* (cat. 3), Mann was not just manipulating the appearance of light. He significantly simplified and strengthened the colour values, with dazzling monochrome yellow flowers complementing the blue interior. By using thick black outlines, he was able to isolate and highlight specific details in his pictures. Much like a jigsaw puzzle, these pictures come together as the sum of a complex, overarching programme. By focusing on the blooms of the dahlias, for example, he was able to intensify their colour, bringing them into sharp relief where a system of subtle tonal gradation, by contrast, would have limited the range and depth of colour. Similarly, in *Mackerel* (c. 1955) (cat. 19), the surface of the fish has been apportioned into nuanced panels of flat colour, and Mann's choice and combination of colours is striking. The fish have been given red faces, blue scales and yellow guts.

Just as with the surface of his directly lit subjects, Mann also experimented with non-naturalistic colour effects in his depiction of shadows. Sometimes they fall like camouflage, manifesting themselves in

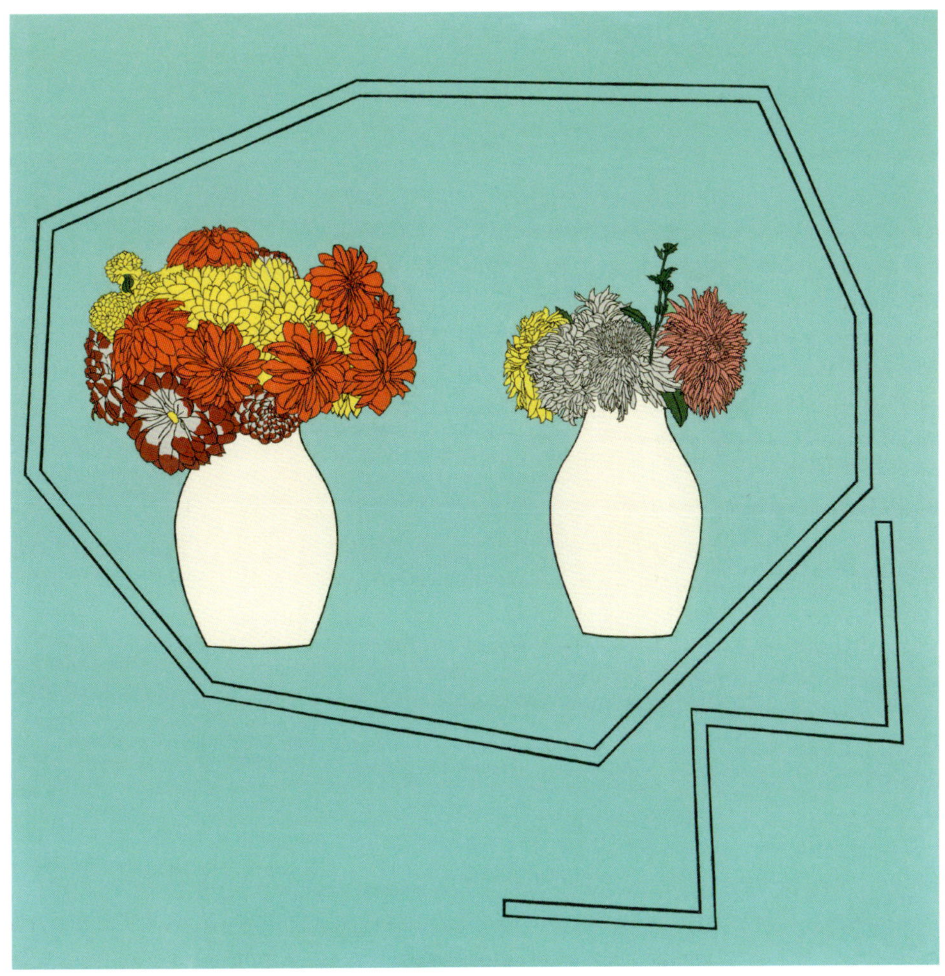

Fig. 4
Patrick Caulfield (1936 – 2005)
Vases of Flowers, 1962

a carefully planned pattern of interlocking colour panels. In *Mackerel*, again, the blade of the knife has been pieced together from brown, grey, blue and yellow patches. In other works, he composed his subjects on a yellow table top, which offered a vivid setting for whatever pieces of fruit or vessels he had to hand. Though he often depicts the edge of the table, in some cases the objects are isolated on the yellow surface with no edges in sight, giving an immediacy and a hallucinogenic quality to the work. In *Still Life with Pomegranate* (c. 1955) (cat. 23), for example, opened and unopened pomegranates alongside two pieces of peel are presented without spatial clues. They appear instead to float over the yellow surface, surrounded by pools of brilliant blue and green shadows.

In many cases, Mann's choice of subject resonated with the new manner of painting that he was developing. He regularly depicted dahlias and anemones during this period, for instance. This choice of flowers was in keeping with the baroque complexity of his carefully pieced-together picture surfaces. Their many petals, delicate structure and brilliant colour lent themselves to the painter's bold artistic experiment. The peeling depths of a pomegranate serve the same purposes as his dahlias. Moreover, it is uncanny that within ten years, Patrick Caulfield had developed a closely similar manner of painting and, what is more, that he even depicted two vases of brilliant flowers, one of which was also filled with dahlias – *Vases of Flowers* (1962, Tate Collection) (fig. 4).

Though there is no direct link, circumstantial or otherwise, between the solid shadow works and those of later artists like Caulfield, the formal similarity is undeniable and striking. The similarity does perhaps speak to some underlying creative need, operative in the decades following the Second World War, to leave aside the involved, turbulent paintings of the immediate post-war years produced by artists in the schools of Paris and New York, such as Jean Fautrier, Pierre Soulages, Jackson Pollock and the like. What is so notable in the case of Cyril Mann is how early he arrived at the same conclusions that many artists only started to draw in the nineteen-sixties and -seventies.

An exhibition of Mann's work to be held at The Lightbox gallery in early 2019, *Cyril Mann: Painter of Light and Shadow*, emphasises the artist's interest in the surface of reality, and the way in which he sought to register the effects of light using paint. In parallel to this interest of Mann's, however, this display of his solid shadow paintings shows another side to his obsession with light. Rather than merely observing and transcribing light, these works show Mann developing an entirely new, non-naturalistic way of representing light and shade. With the inspiration of a bare lightbulb throwing sharp, impenetrable shadows, he was emboldened to make paintings that reveal the structure of their composition.

With his sharp outlines and the dense curtain of shadow clearly marked out, these works defy the accepted norms of representation that operated in the halls of British painting in the nineteen-fifties. Indeed, his works are so uncharacteristic of their period that they are better contextualised amongst visual art made in the following decades, rather than those by his direct contemporaries. In short, these works are vivid and excitingly anachronistic, posing an as yet unanswered question for the histories of post-war British art.

*

Mann's solid shadow style went as quickly as it came. Some time after moving into the small, lightless flat at Old Street, Mann's solid shadow paintings were discovered by Erica Brausen, the proprietor of the Hanover Gallery. She sought to promote and sell them, offering him a solo exhibition if he could produce enough work to fill her gallery. Mann's circumstances changed, however, when the local council rehoused him, moving him from the dark flat in Paul Street to brighter accommodation at Bevin Court, Islington, whereupon the sharp-edged shadows disappeared from his work.

Once more, with a change of accommodation, Mann's style changed entirely. As Russell Taylor has written, '[t]his style was applied strictly for only a year or two [...]. But then it gradually became softened around the edges, as though its constraints were too limiting for him'.[4] The reason for this change was in fact a change of address, and the readmission of light into the space where Mann lived and worked. Though glimpses of his solid shadow manner recur in subsequent decades of his career, his rigorous shadows and electric colouring were fleeting – a moment of stylised, graphic aplomb in the midst of a career dedicated to naturalism.

A small, corresponding display of work by Patrick Caulfield, John Wesley, Michael Craig-Martin and Euan Uglow highlights a certain stylistic continuity in post-war Anglo-American art, as well as hinting to an analogy between these artists' work and the solid shadow paintings of Cyril Mann. Rather than making a firm, art historical claim about the lineage of the later artists' work, the display intends humbly to introduce this shared style – a playful, intriguing and visually coherent group of art.

Postscriptum

To date, no thematic history has been written about artists working in a highly stylised, representational manner after the Second World War. The work of Patrick Caulfield, Michael Craig-Martin, John Wesley, Tom Wesselmann and, more recently, Julian Opie has not been openly acknowledged as a stylistically coherent and conceptually related corpus. Though the similarities between these artists' work is widely known, and though the Tate recently addressed Caulfield's work in relation to that of Gary Hume, no firm historical basis has been given to this visual, seemingly superficial continuity.

The work itself holds a clue to why this may be. Working with bold outlines, attenuated silhouettes and exaggerated colour, these artists have placed a high value on a wordless simplicity. Though underpinned by complex materialist analyses of post-industrial capitalism, especially in the case of Craig-Martin, these artists' works vividly reject the pretentions of concept-driven artistic creativity. As Marco Livingstone has written of John Wesley's work, in all these artists' output there is 'a truce between high art and low culture'.[5] The retention of representation is notable in this respect, and though each artist has their own distinctive graphic schemas, the common thread that brings their work together is a rigorous, imaginative simplification of their pictorial subjects.

Certain still-life paintings by Euan Uglow may also be related to this group, with their flamboyant colouring, exacting compositions and visible pencil outlines. The most complete works give the impression of fruit or flowers that have been pinned to the canvas. Like the aforementioned artists, Uglow's project was to relate his subject in the purest of visual terms possible. His creative urge was tightly bound-up with a desire to observe and imitate what he could see. Indeed, in all of these artists' work, intensive looking has bestowed a dazzling, unnatural vibrancy on their pictures. The relationship between representation and stylisation in these works is vexed and ambiguous, a topic of lasting interest.

Endnotes

1. Mark Hudson, 'Cyril Mann's post-war cityscapes' in Mark Hudson and Veronica Cecil, *St Paul's from Moor Lane*, 2011, Sylph Editions/Piano Nobile.
2. In conversation with the author.
3. John Russell Taylor, *The Sun is God: The Life and Work of Cyril Mann*, 1999, Lund Humphries, p. 31.
4. Ibid., p. 31.
5. Marco Livingstone, 'Try a Little Tenderness', *John Wesley: Works on Paper & Paintings*, 2008, Waddington Galleries, p. 5.

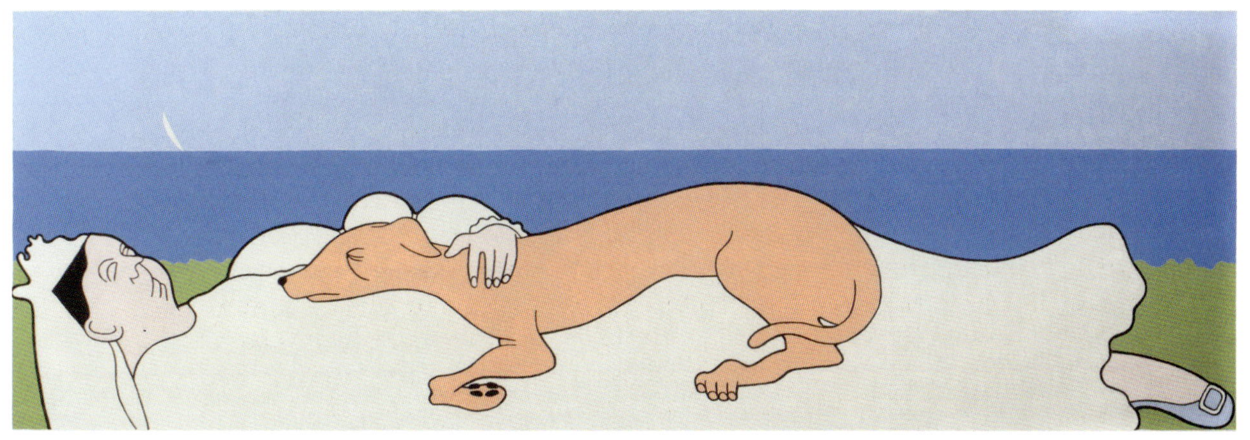

Fig.5
John Wesley (b. 1928)
Queen Victoria at Rest, 1989

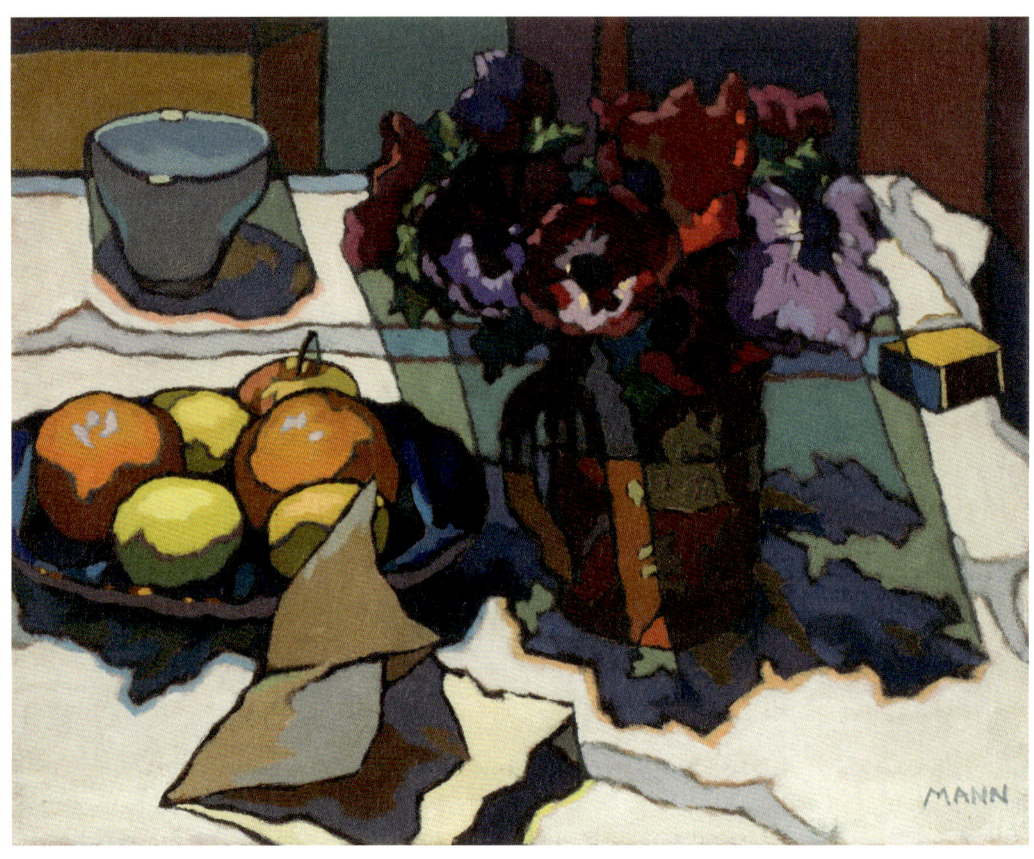

1.

Still Life of Anemones, c.1951

Signed lower right 'MANN'
Oil on canvas
39.4 × 50.3 cm / 15½ × 19¾ in

Provenance
The Artist's Estate

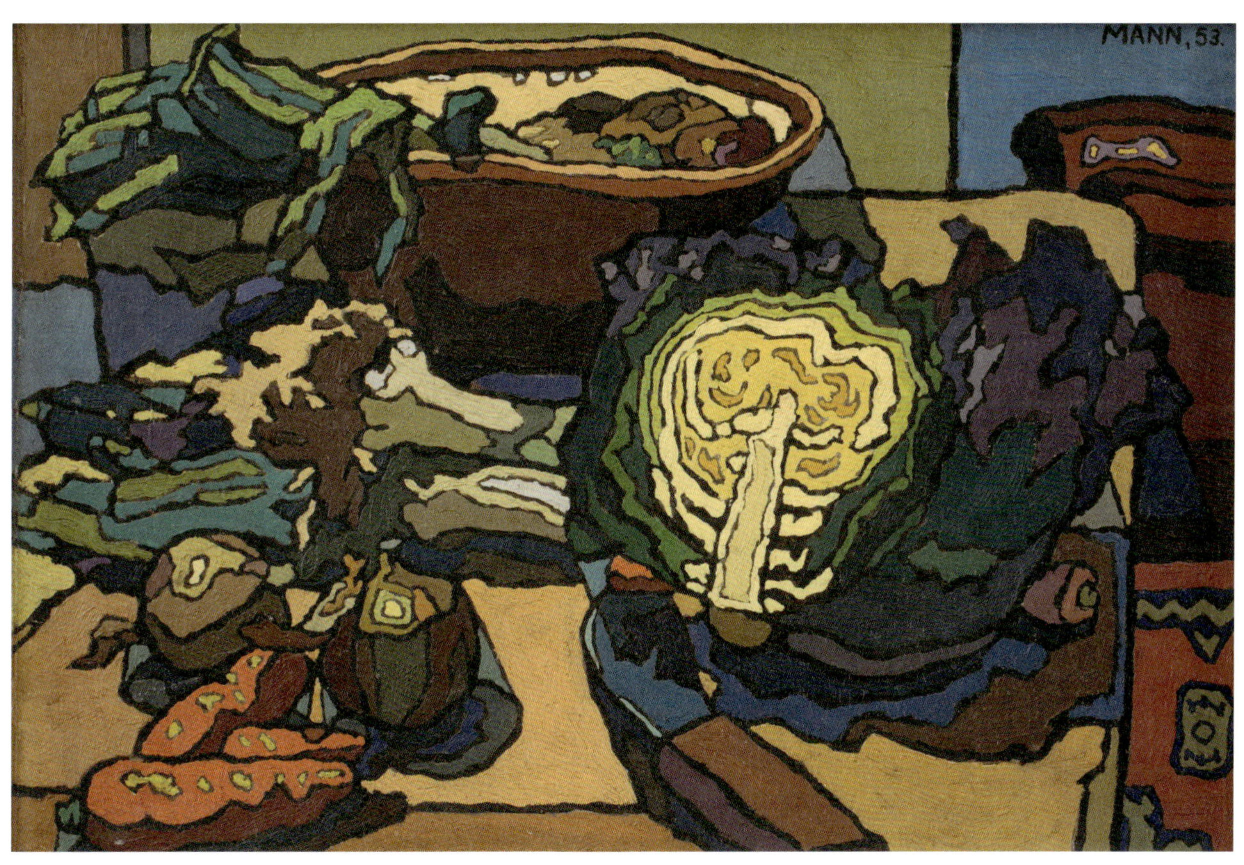

2.

Still Life with Cabbage, 1953

Signed upper right 'MANN, 53.'
Oil on board
33 × 49.5 cm / 13 × 19½ in

Provenance
The Artist's Estate

3.

Dahlias in Blue Vase, c.1953

Signed upper left 'MANN'
Oil on canvas
46.5 × 54.5 cm / 17½ × 22¼ in

Provenance
The Artist's Estate

Literature
John Russell Taylor, *The Sun is God: The Life and Work of Cyril Mann*, 1999, Lund Humphries, p. 98

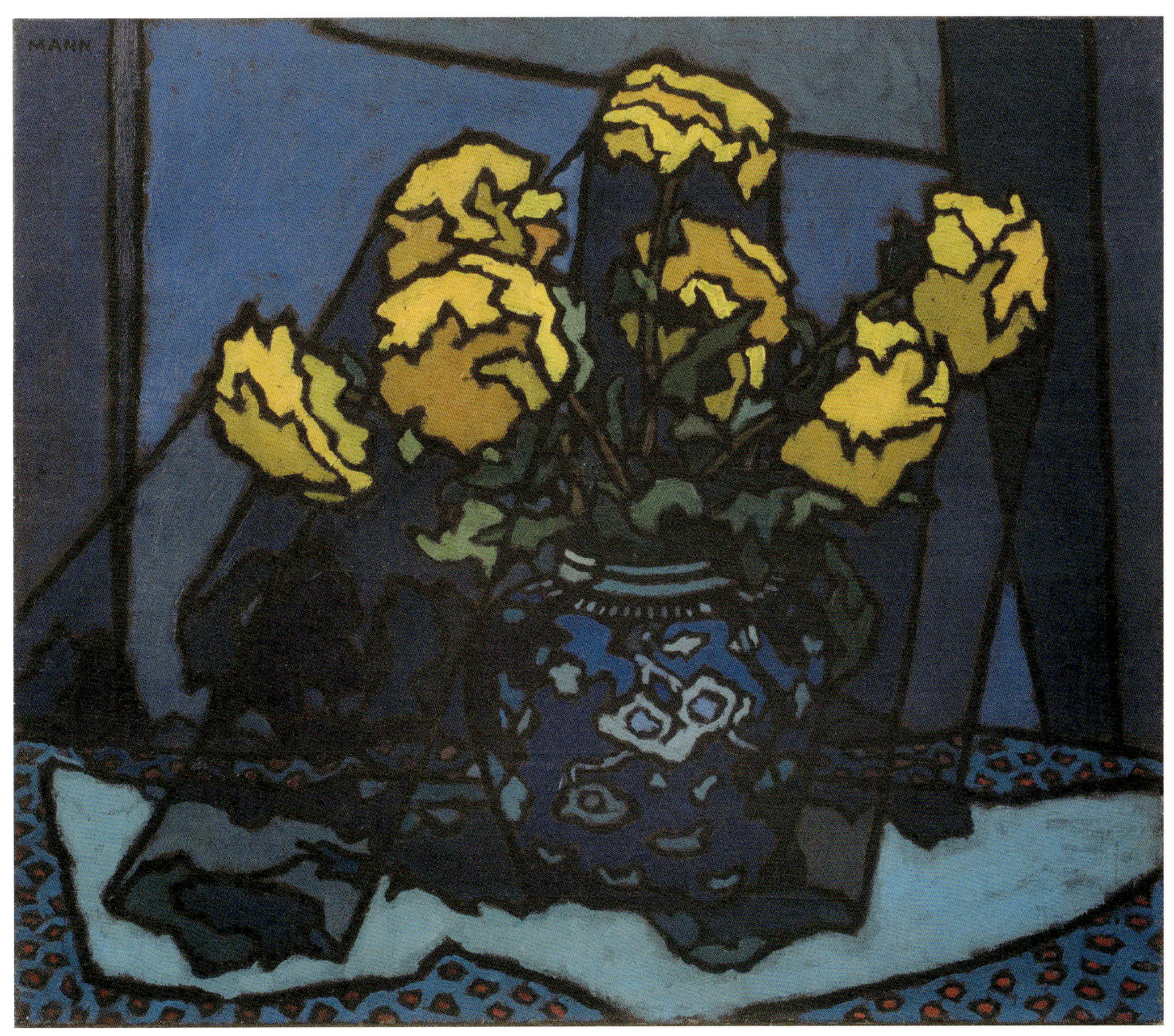
MANN

4.

The White Rose, c.1955

Signed lower right 'MANN'
Inscribed label on verso ''THE WHITE ROSE'/Cyril Mann'
Oil on board
42.5 × 18.3 cm / 16¾ × 7¼ in

Provenance
Charles Glen Robson
Amanda Mann

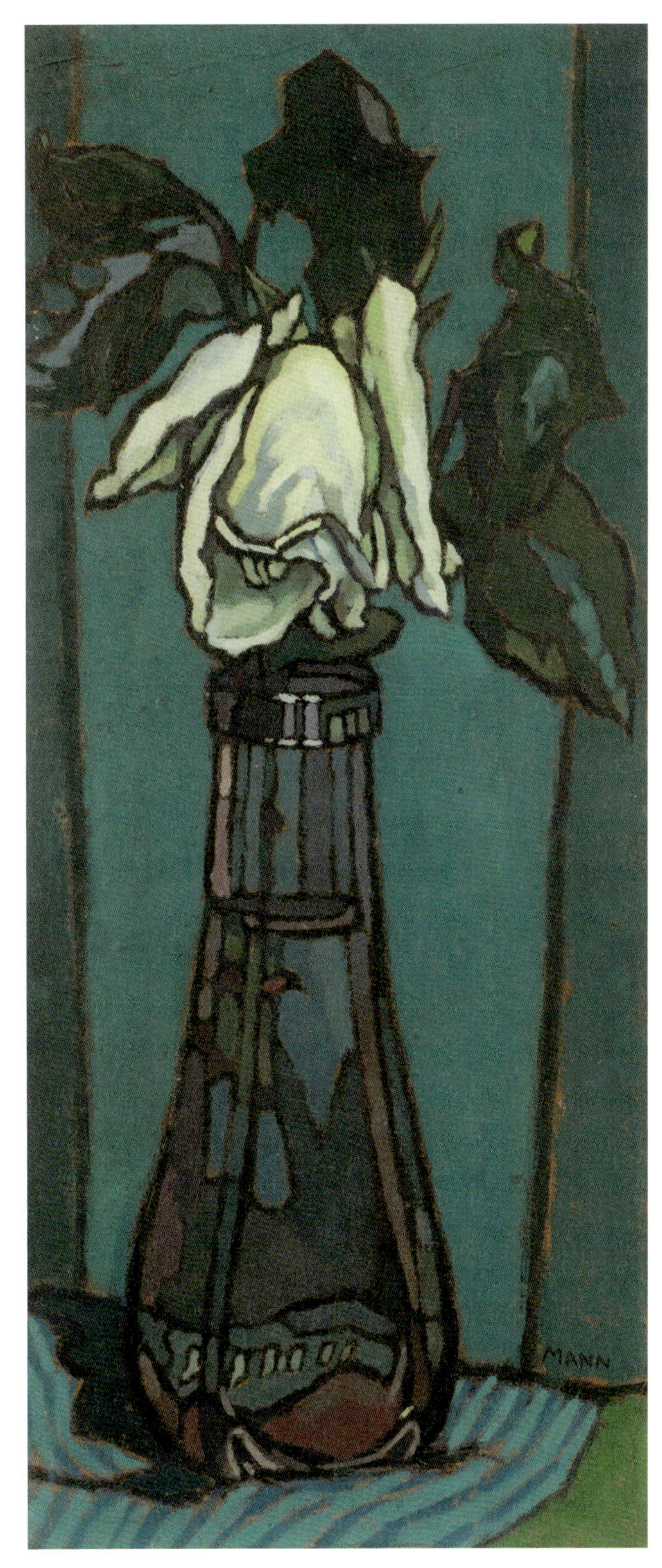
MANN

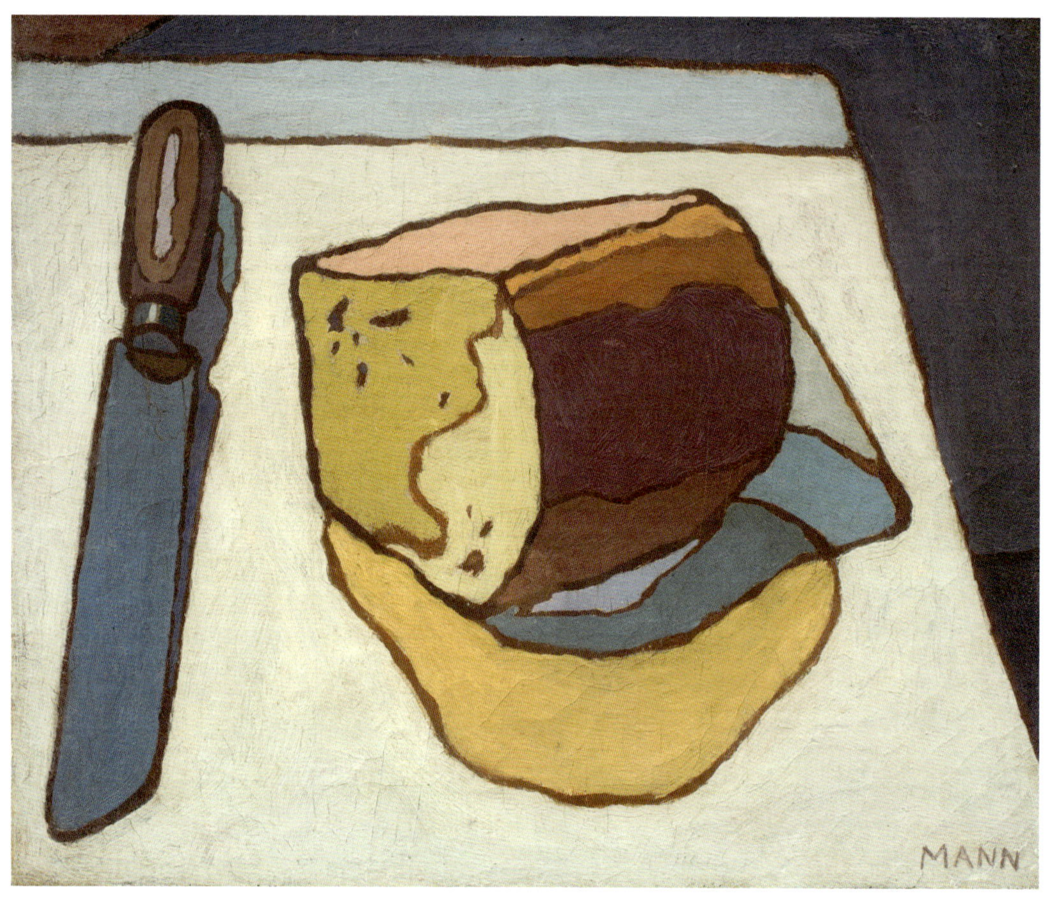

5.

Bread and Knife, c.1955

Signed lower right 'MANN'
Oil on canvas
22.7 × 27.7 cm / 9 × 10⅞ in

Provenance
The Artist's Estate

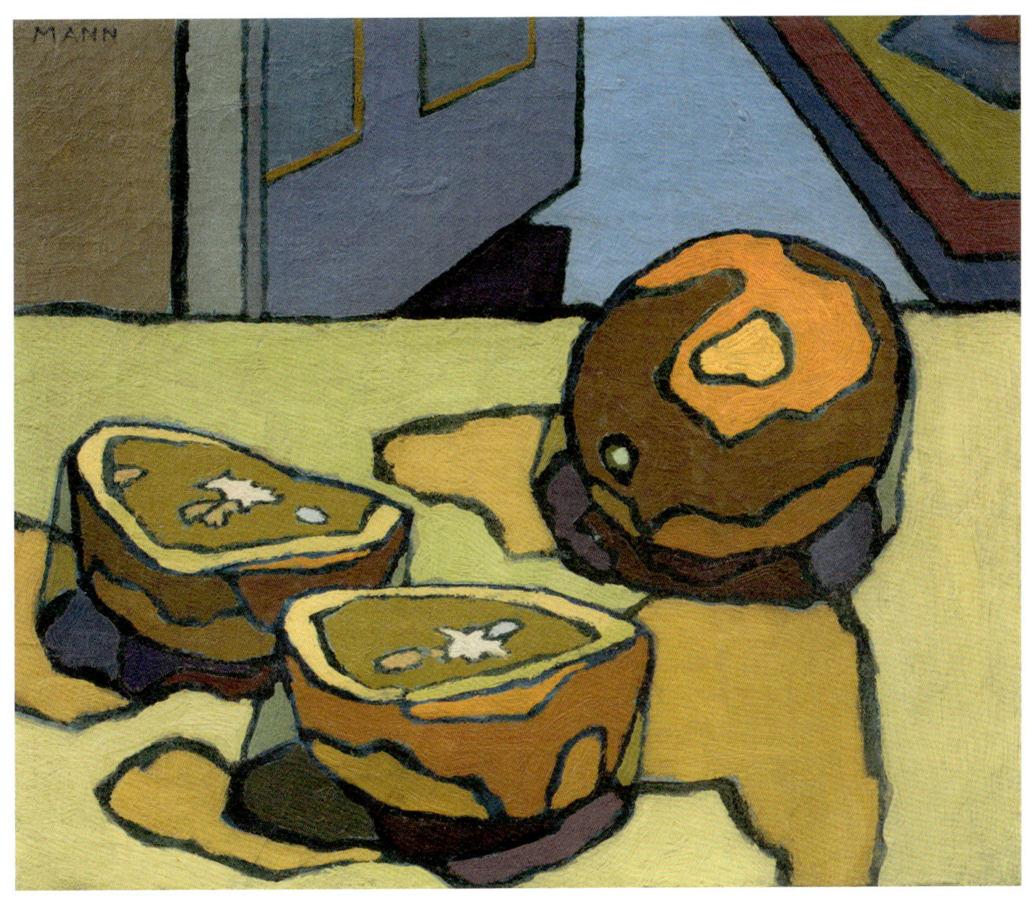

6.

Still Life, c.1955

Signed upper left 'MANN'
Inscribed on verso 'CYRIL MANN Still Life 15 gns.'
Oil on canvas
22.7 × 27.7 cm / 9 × 10⅞ in

Provenance
The Artist's Estate

7.

Dish of Fruit, c.1955

Inscribed label on verso 'No. 2. "Dish of Fruit"/Cyril Mann. 15 gns.'
Inscribed on verso 'Hanover Gallery' and 'Bowl S. Lighter [illegible]/ Oranges and [illegible]'
Oil on canvasboard
25 × 36 cm / 9⅞ × 14⅛ in

Provenance
The Artist's Estate

Literature
John Russell Taylor, *The Sun is God: The Life and Work of Cyril Mann*, 1999, Lund Humphries, p. 89

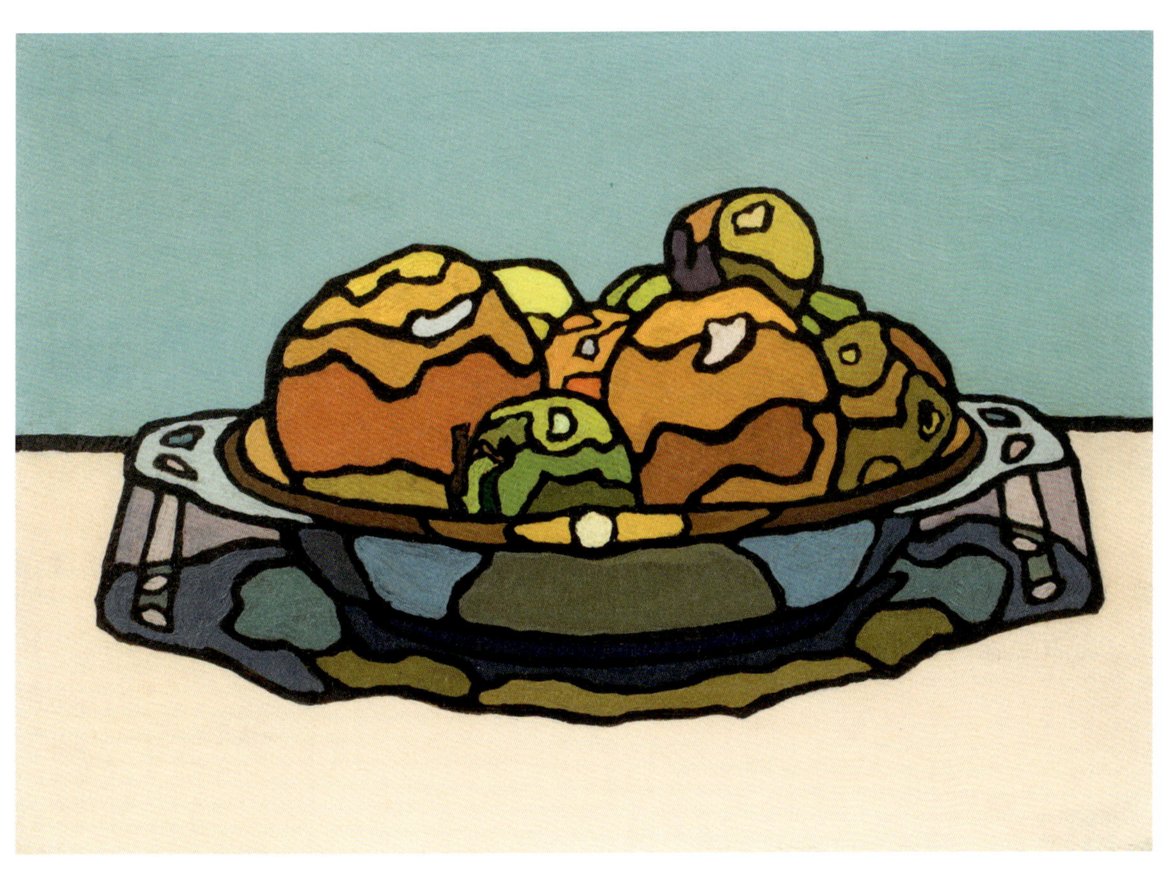

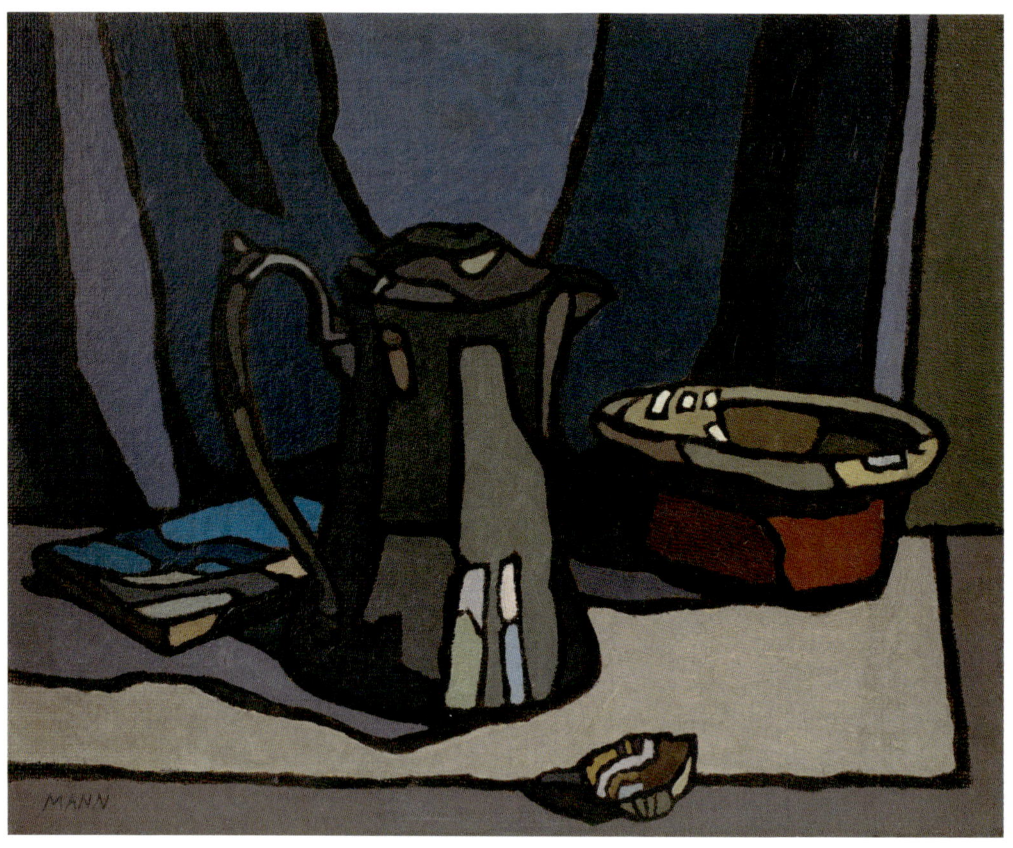

8.

Still Life with Pewter Jug, c.1955

Signed lower left 'MANN'
Oil on canvasboard
31.7 × 40 cm / 12½ × 15¾ in

Provenance
The Artist's Estate

Literature
John Russell Taylor, *The Sun is God: The Life and Work of Cyril Mann*, 1999, Lund Humphries, p. 94

9.

Still Life with Bottles, c.1955

Oil on board
41.6 × 33.3 cm / 16⅜ × 13⅛ in

Provenance
The Artist's Estate

Literature
John Russell Taylor, *The Sun is God: The Life and Work of Cyril Mann*, 1999, Lund Humphries, p. 94

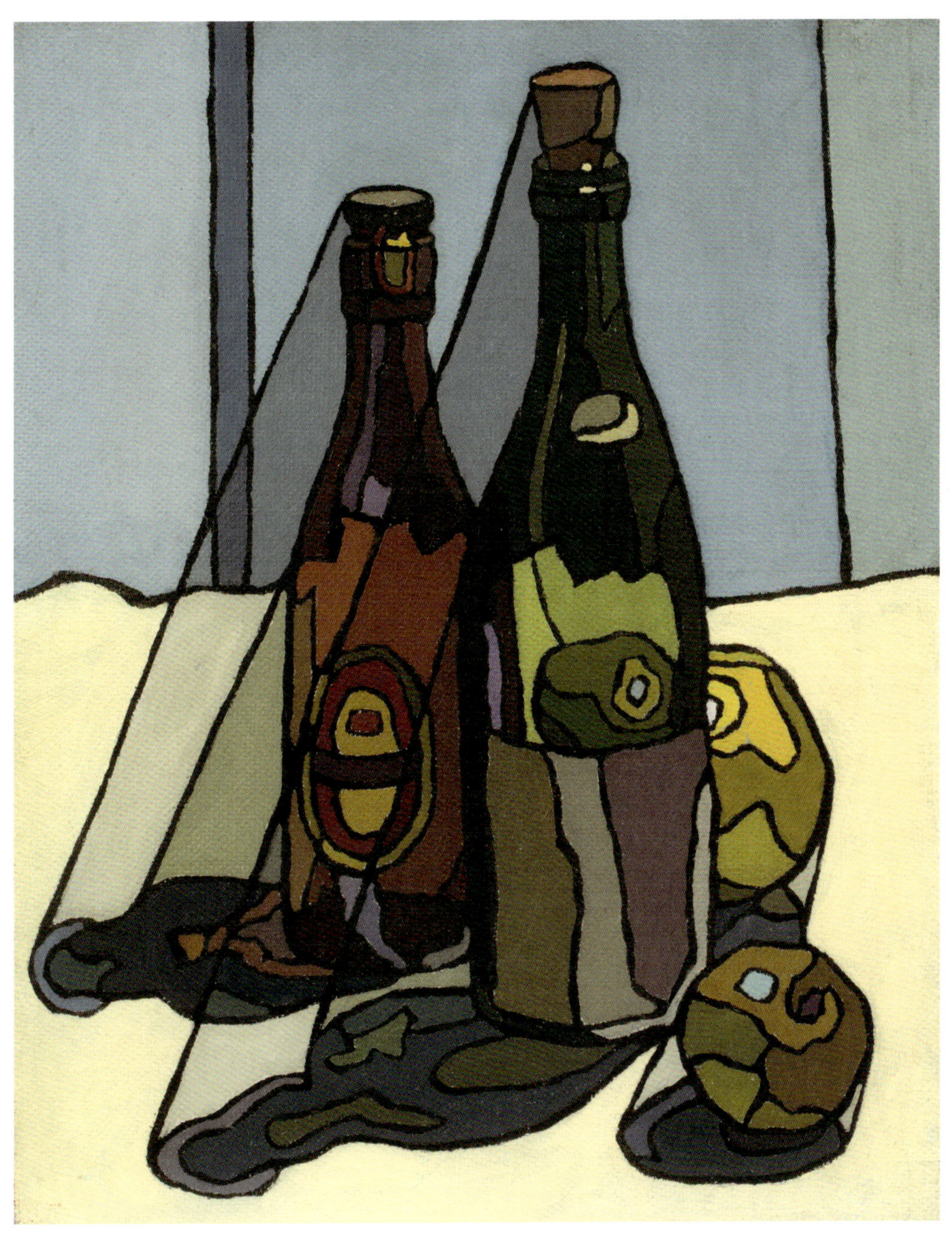

10.

Peeled Apple, c.1955

Signed lower right 'MANN"
Inscribed label on verso ''Peeled apple'/ 9 gns/ Cyril Mann.'
Oil on board
15 × 24 cm / 5⅞ × 9½ in

Provenance
The Artist's Estate

Literature
John Russell Taylor, *The Sun is God: The Life and Work of Cyril Mann*, 1999, Lund Humphries, p. 88

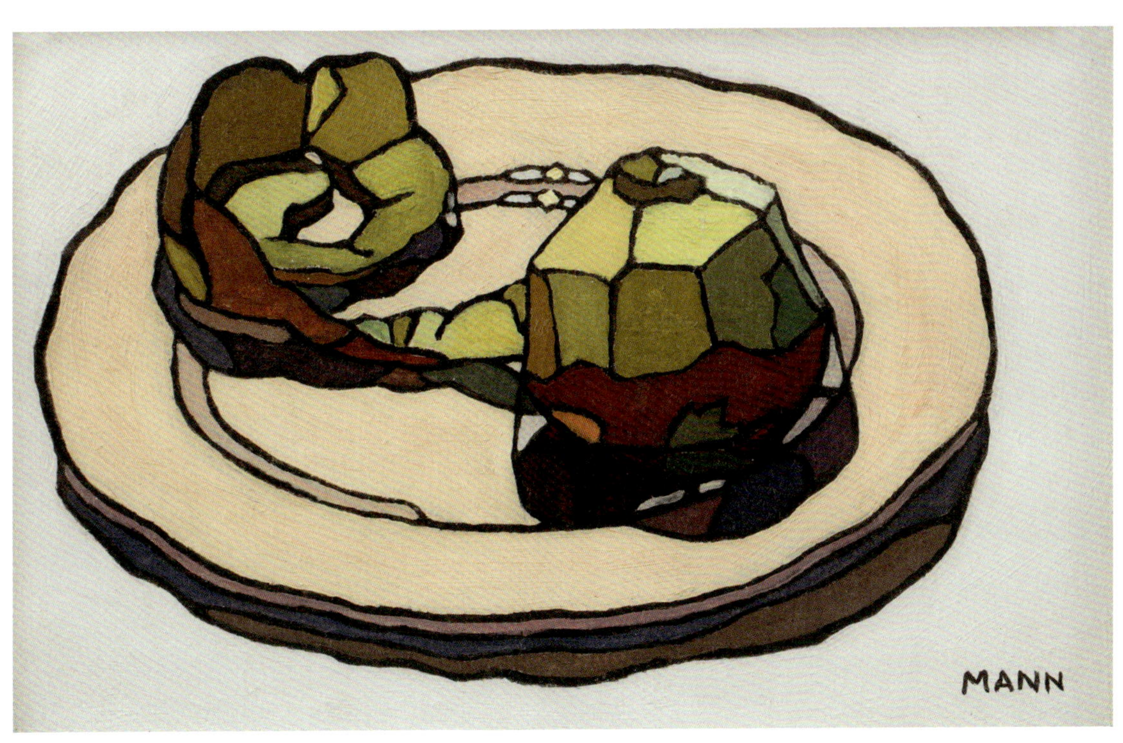
MANN

11.

Solid Shadow Studies of Fruit, c.1955

Charcoal and watercolour on paper
31.5 × 44.8 cm / 12⅜ × 17⅝ in

Provenance
The Artist's Estate

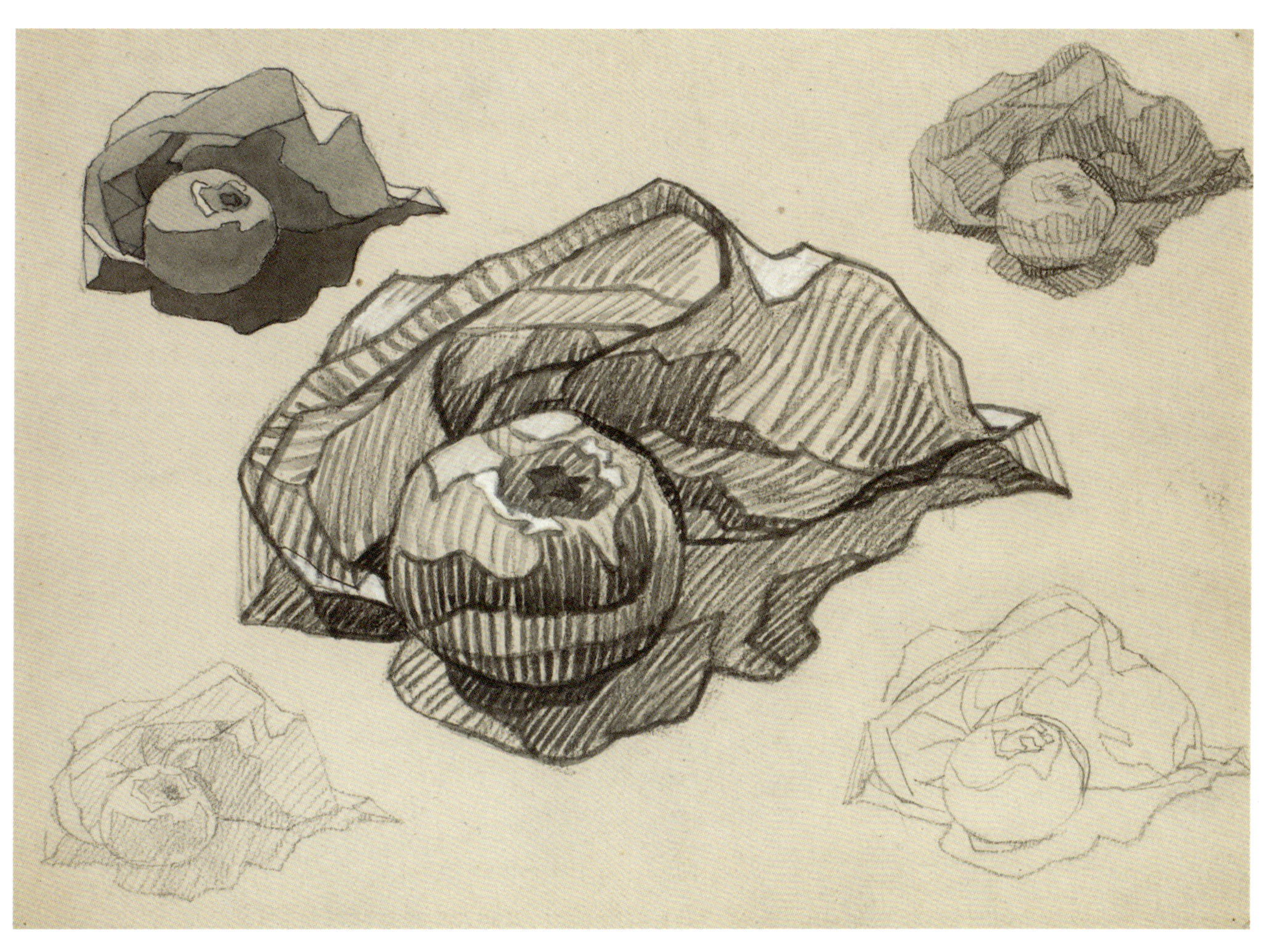

12.

Orange and Grape, c.1955

Signed upper left 'MANN'
Oil on board
14 × 29 cm / 5½ × 11⅜ in

Provenance
The Artist's Estate

Literature
John Russell Taylor, *The Sun is God: The Life and Work of Cyril Mann*, 1999, Lund Humphries, p. 89

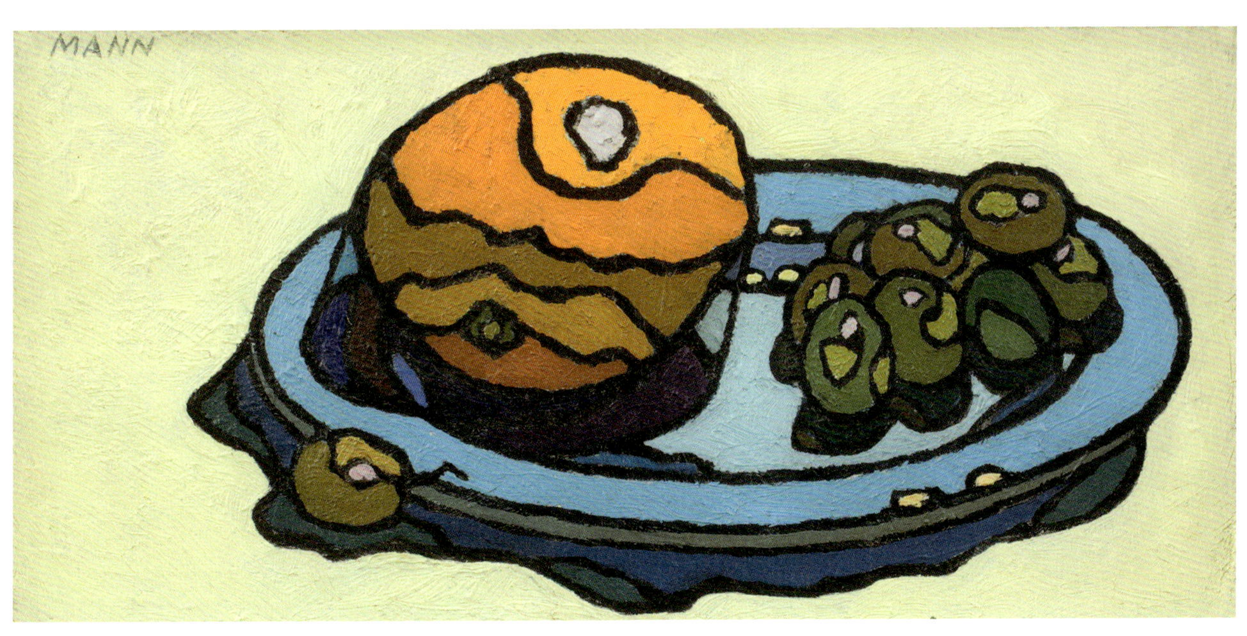
MANN

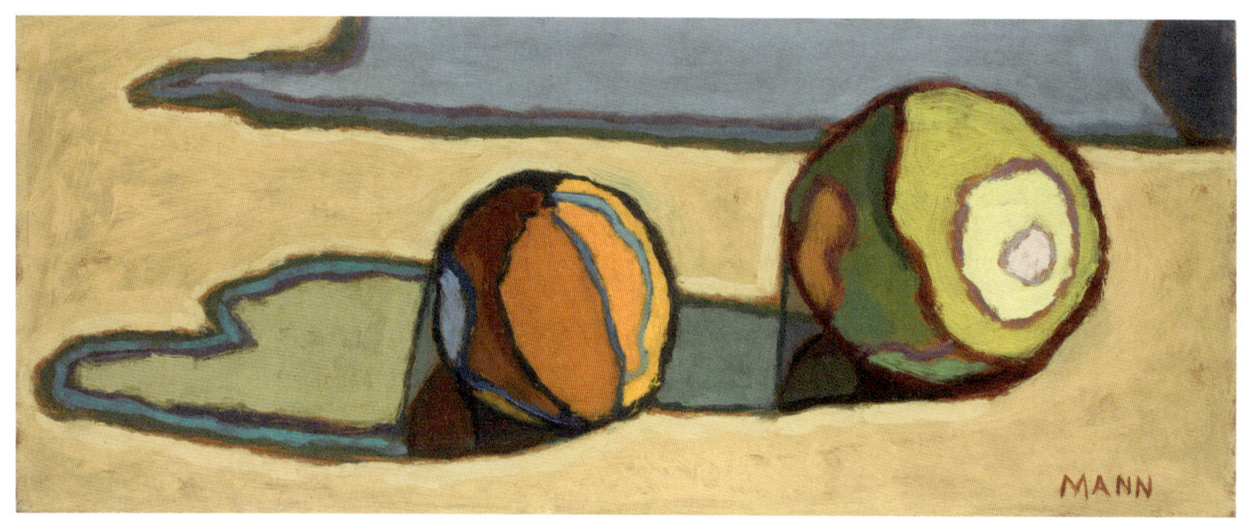

13.

Still Life of Fruit, c.1955

Signed lower right 'MANN'
Oil on board
16.2 × 41.1 cm / 6⅜ × 16⅛ in

Provenance
The Artist's Estate

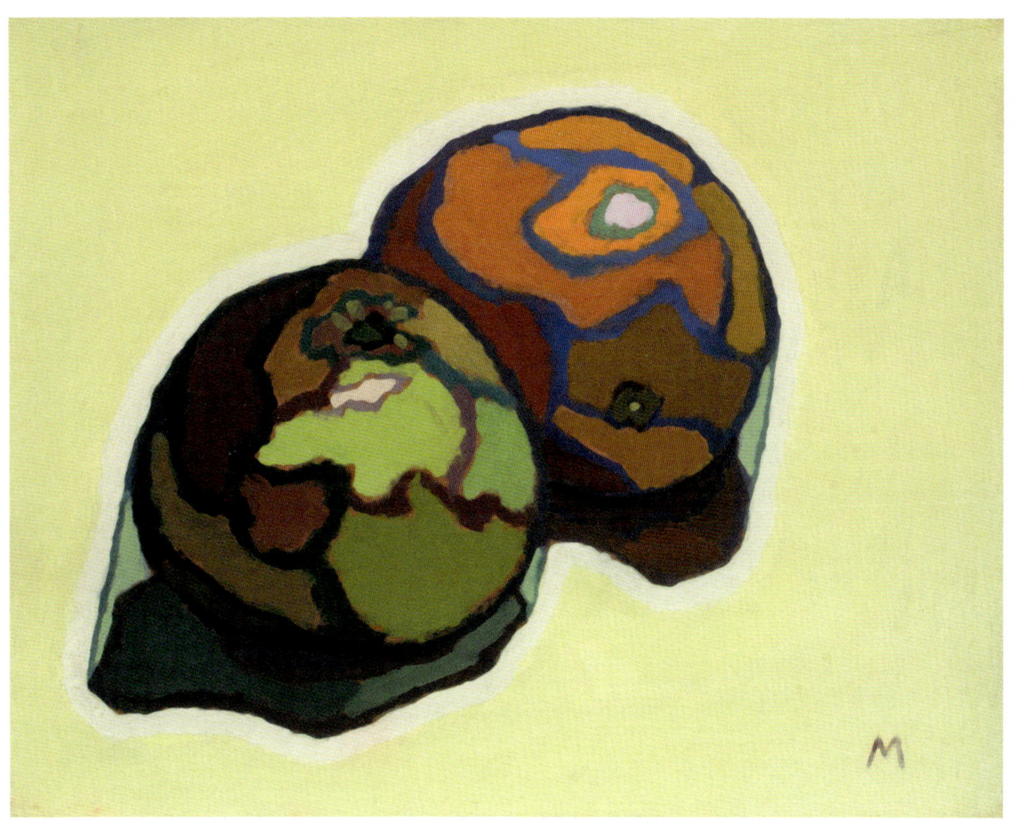

14.

Apple and Orange, c.1955

Signed lower right 'M'
Oil on board
20 × 25 cm / 7⅞ × 9⅞ in

Provenance
The Artist's Estate

15.

Still Life of Bottle and Jug, c.1955

Signed on verso 'Cyril Mann'
Oil on board
44.5 × 31 cm / 17½ × 12¼ in

Provenance
The Artist's Estate

Literature
John Russell Taylor, *The Sun is God: The Life and Work of Cyril Mann*, 1999, Lund Humphries, p. 91

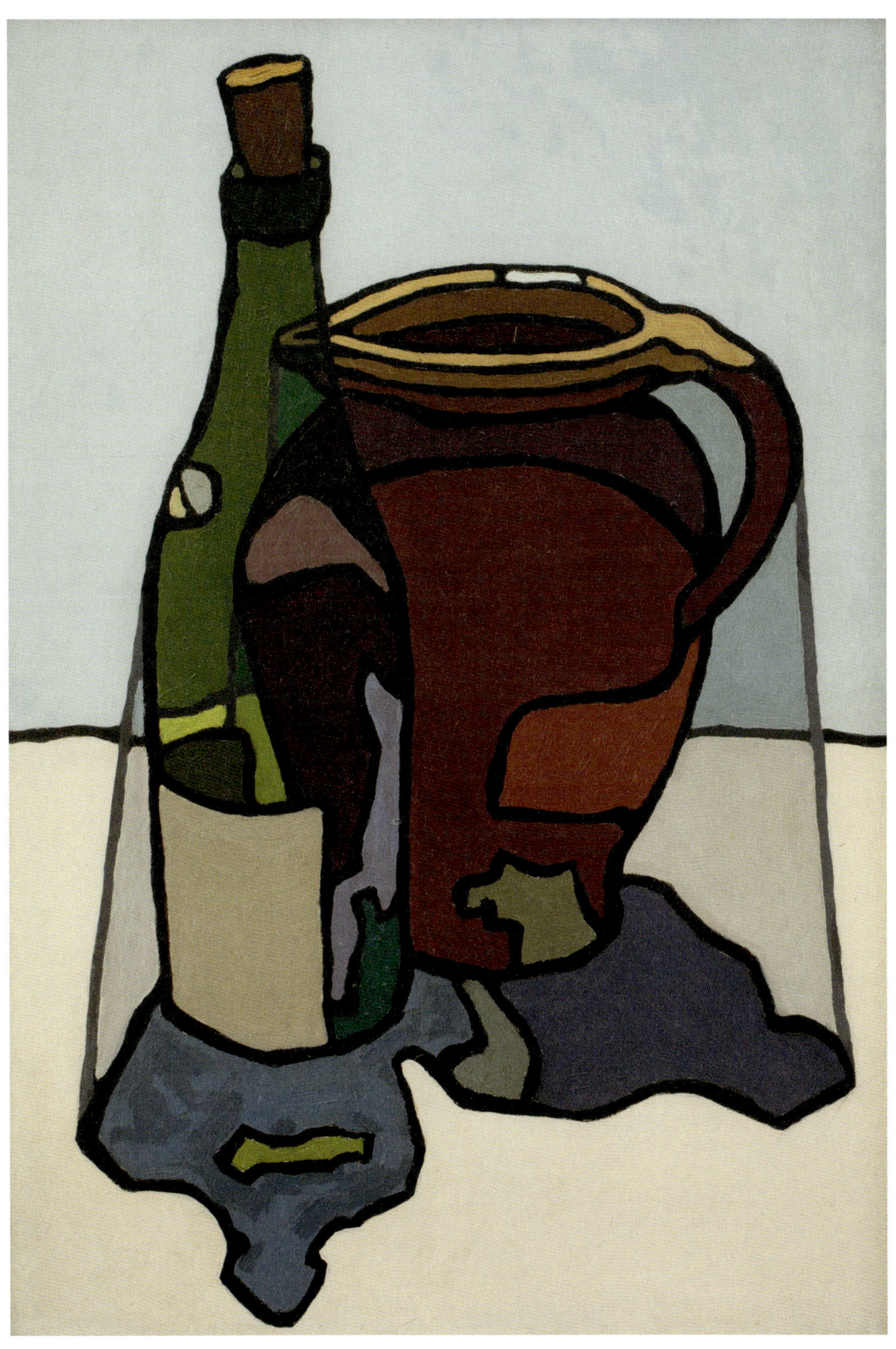

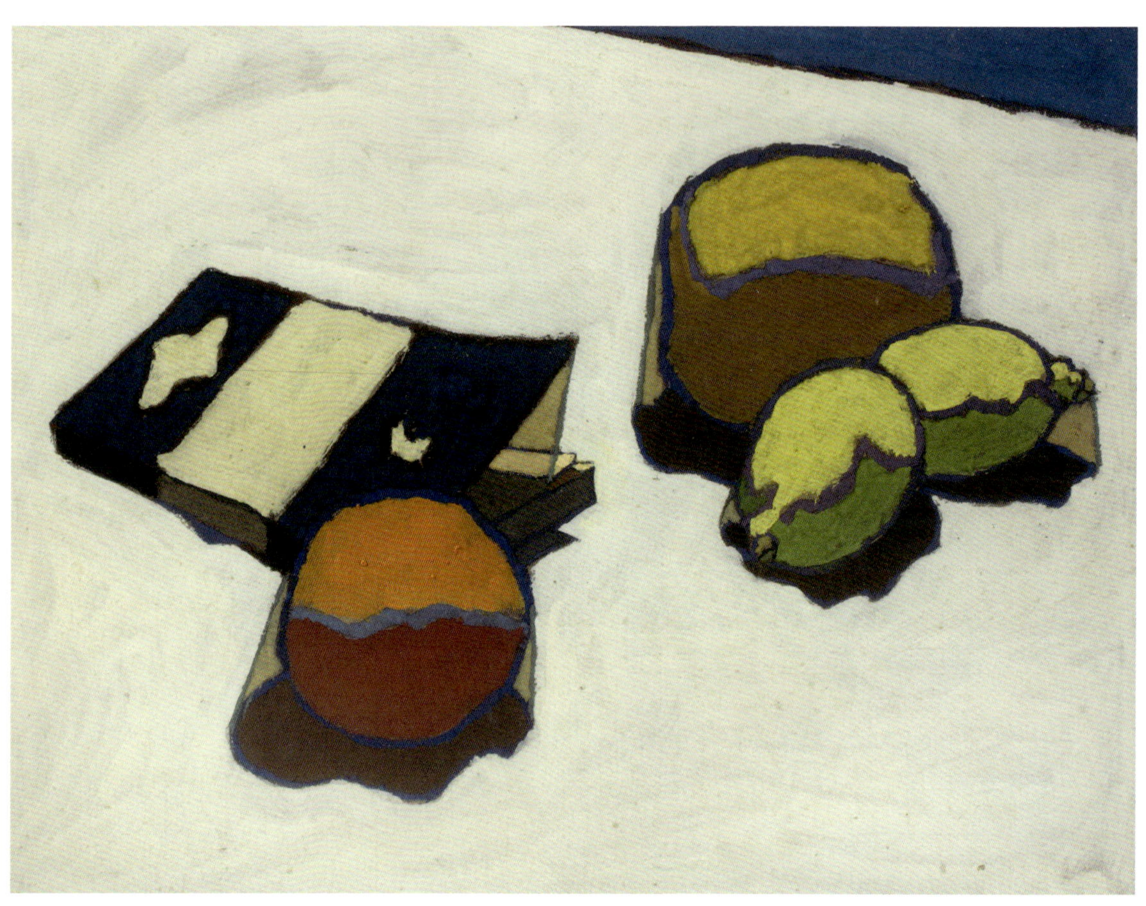

16.

Still Life with Book, c.1955

Oil on paper
30 × 40 cm / 11¾ × 15¾ in

Provenance
The Artist's Estate

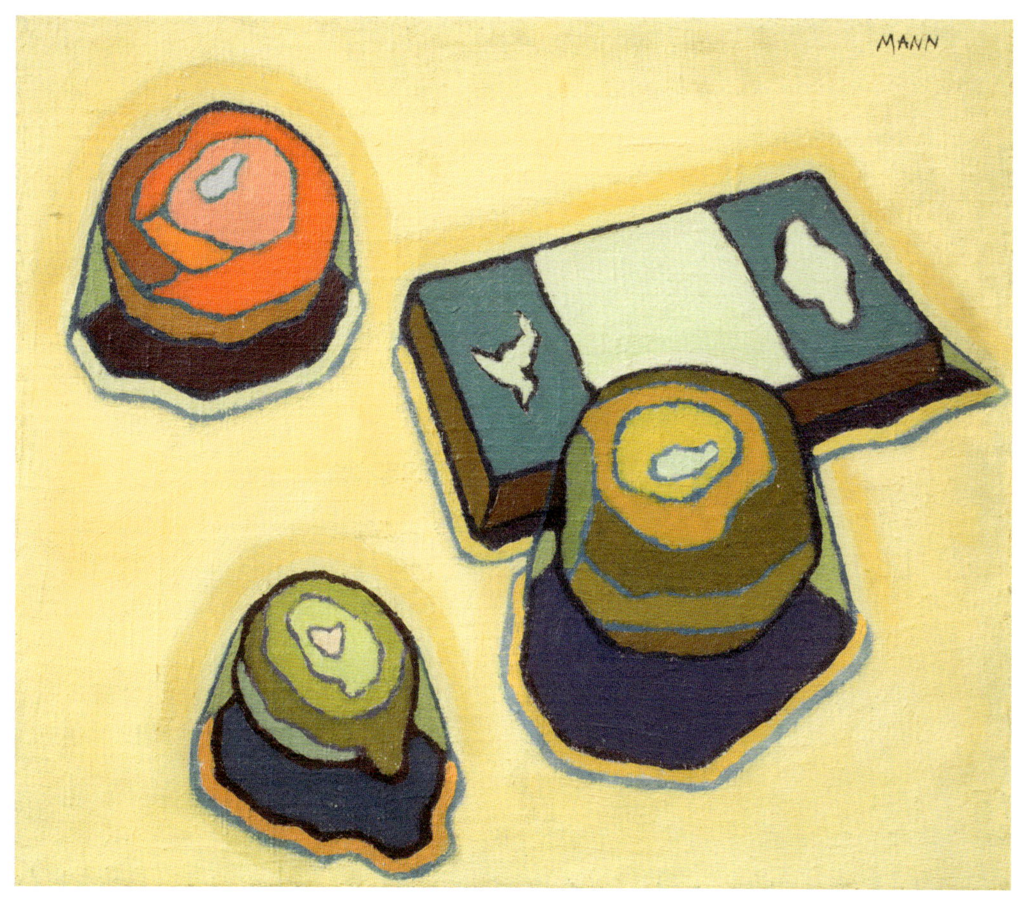

17.

Pelican Book and Fruit, c.1955

Signed upper right 'MANN'
Oil on canvas
30.5 × 37 cm / 12⅛ × 14⅝ in

Provenance
The Artist's Estate

Literature
John Russell Taylor, *The Sun is God: The Life and Work of Cyril Mann,* 1999, Lund Humphries, p. 97

18.

Two Jugs, c.1956

Signed lower right 'M'
Oil on board
40.5 × 30.5 cm / 16 × 12⅛ in

Provenance
The Artist's Estate

Literature
John Russell Taylor, *The Sun is God: The Life and Work of Cyril Mann*, 1999, Lund Humphries, p. 95

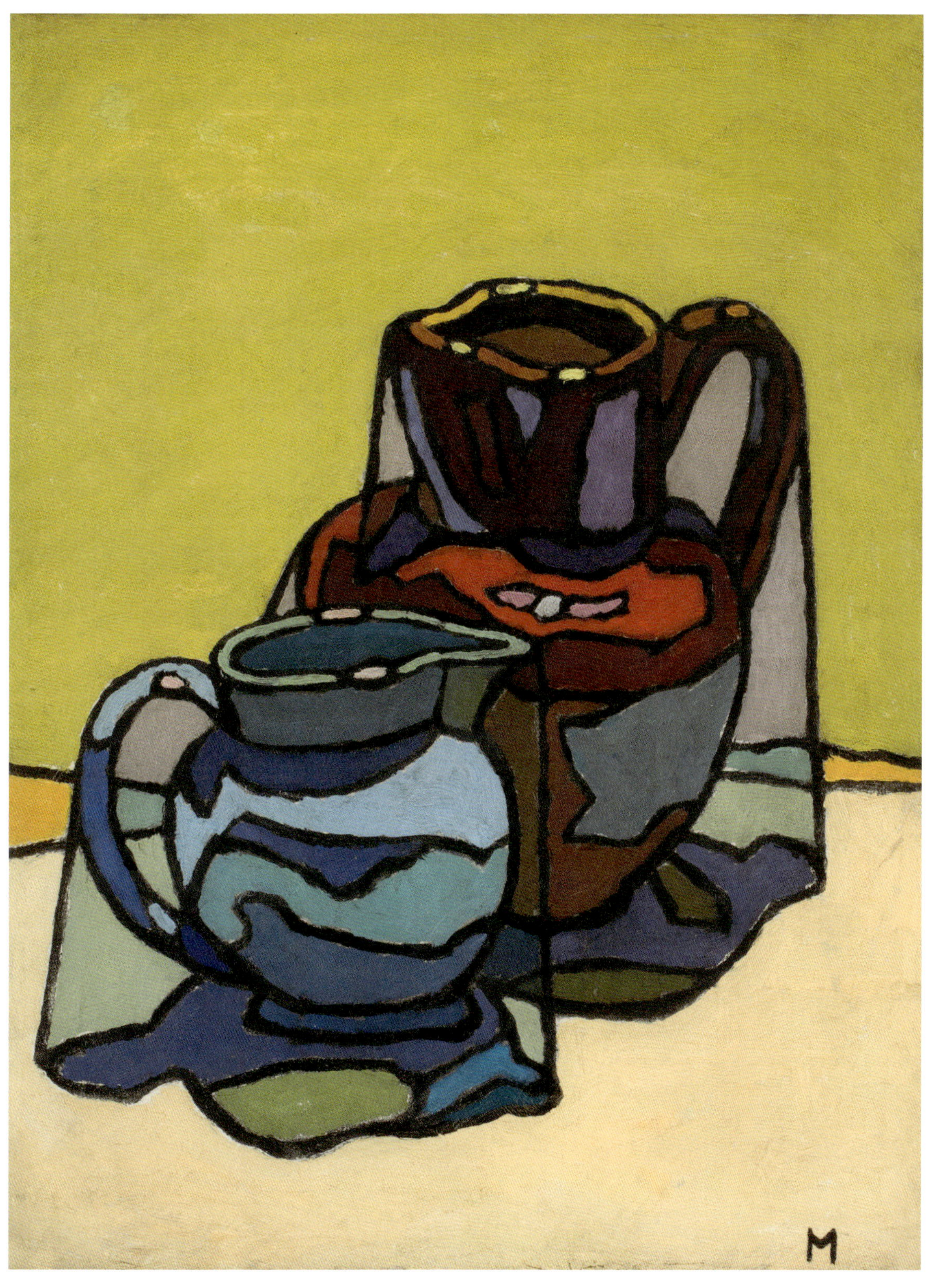
M

19.

Mackerel, c.1956

Oil on board
30.5 × 35.6 cm / 12⅛ × 14⅛ in

Provenance
The Artist's Estate

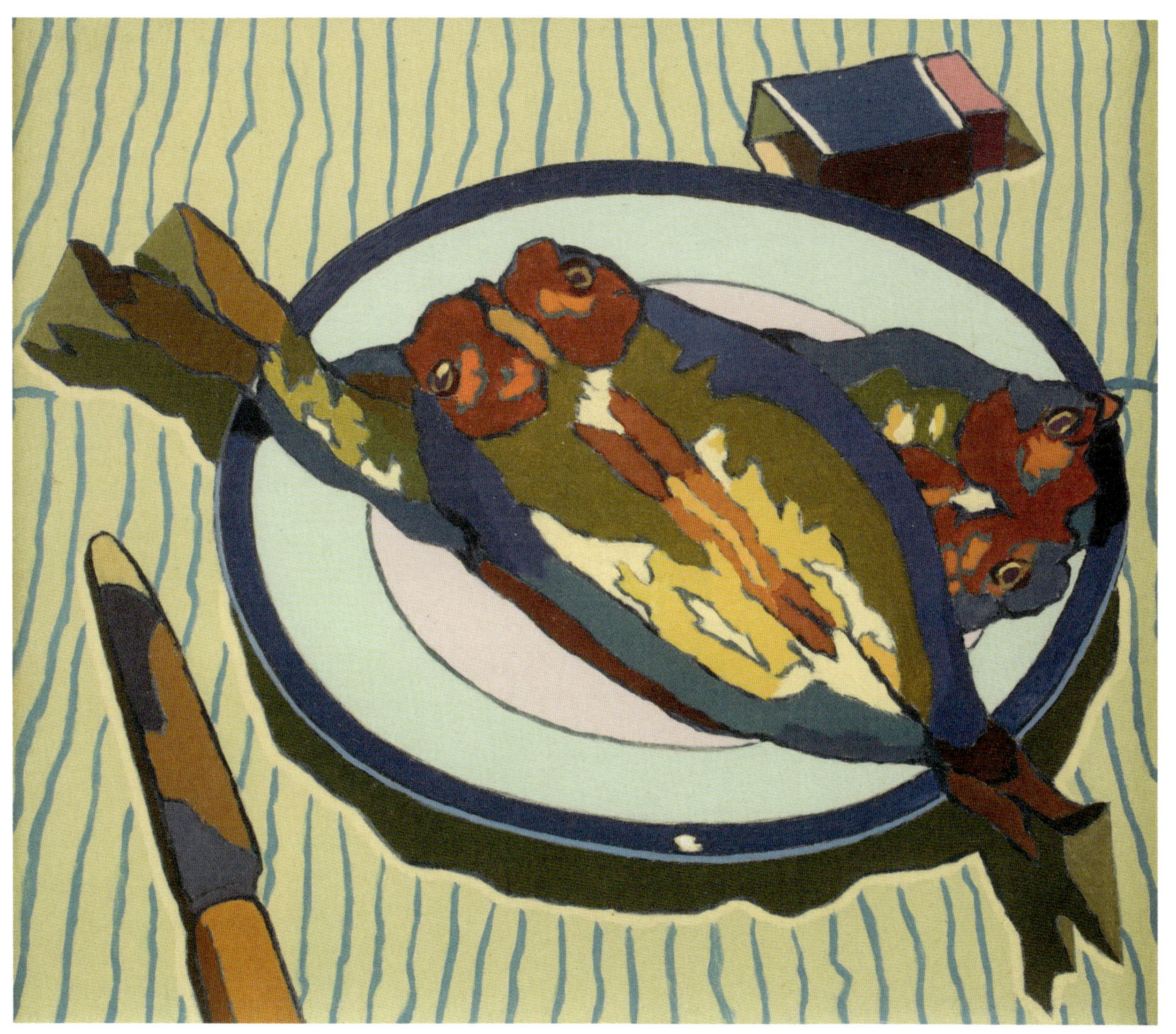

20.

Still Life with Mug, c.1956

Inscribed on stretcher 'no. 6'
Oil on canvas
35.5 × 45.7 cm / 14 × 18 in

Provenance
The Artist's Estate

Literature
John Russell Taylor, *The Sun is God: The Life and Work of Cyril Mann*, 1999, Lund Humphries, p. 96

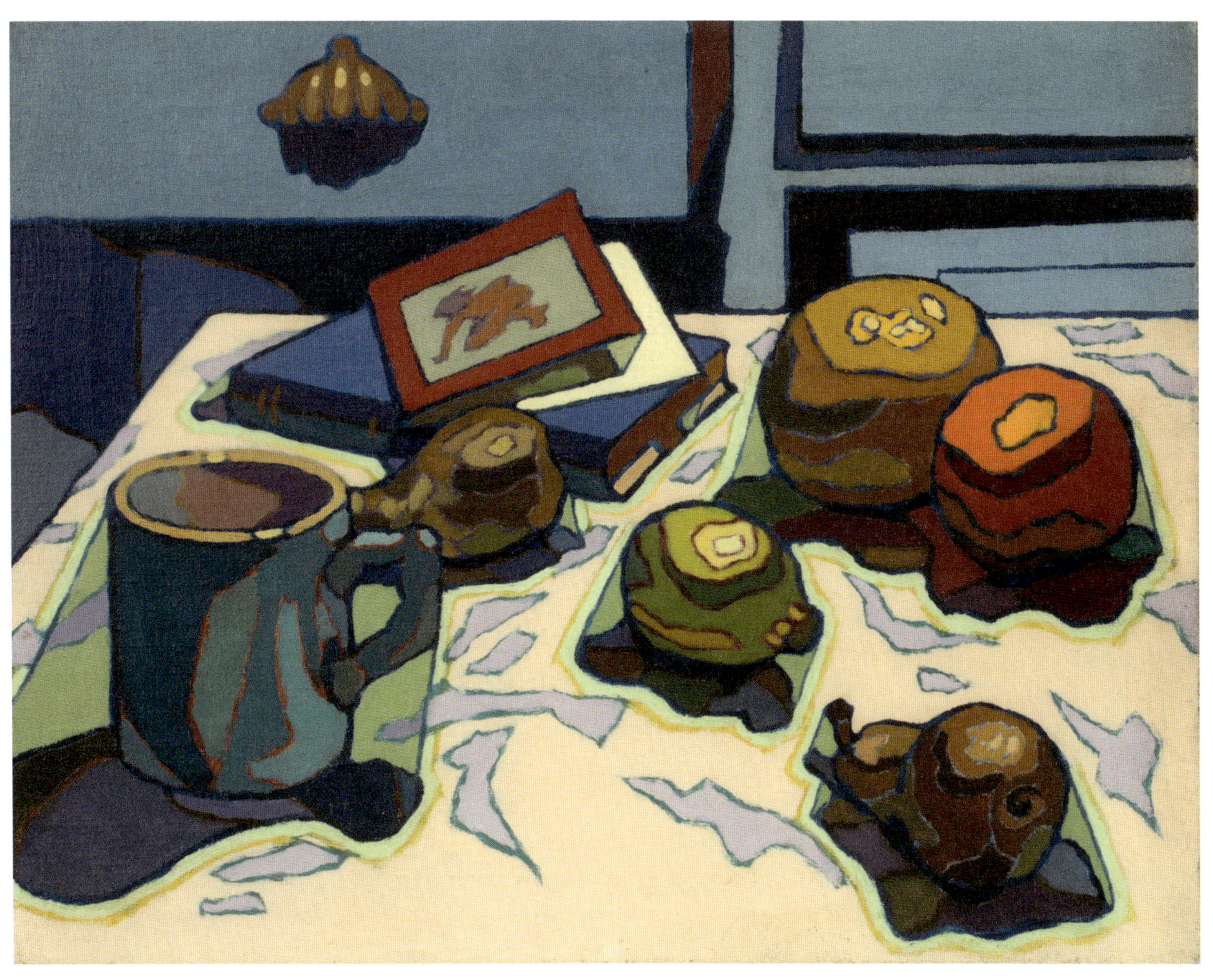

21.

Still Life with Fruit, 1956

Signed upper right 'MANN 56'
Oil on canvas
35.8 × 45.5 cm / 14⅛ × 17⅞ in

Provenance
The Artist's Estate

Literature
John Russell Taylor, *The Sun is God: The Life and Work of Cyril Mann*, 1999, Lund Humphries, p. 96

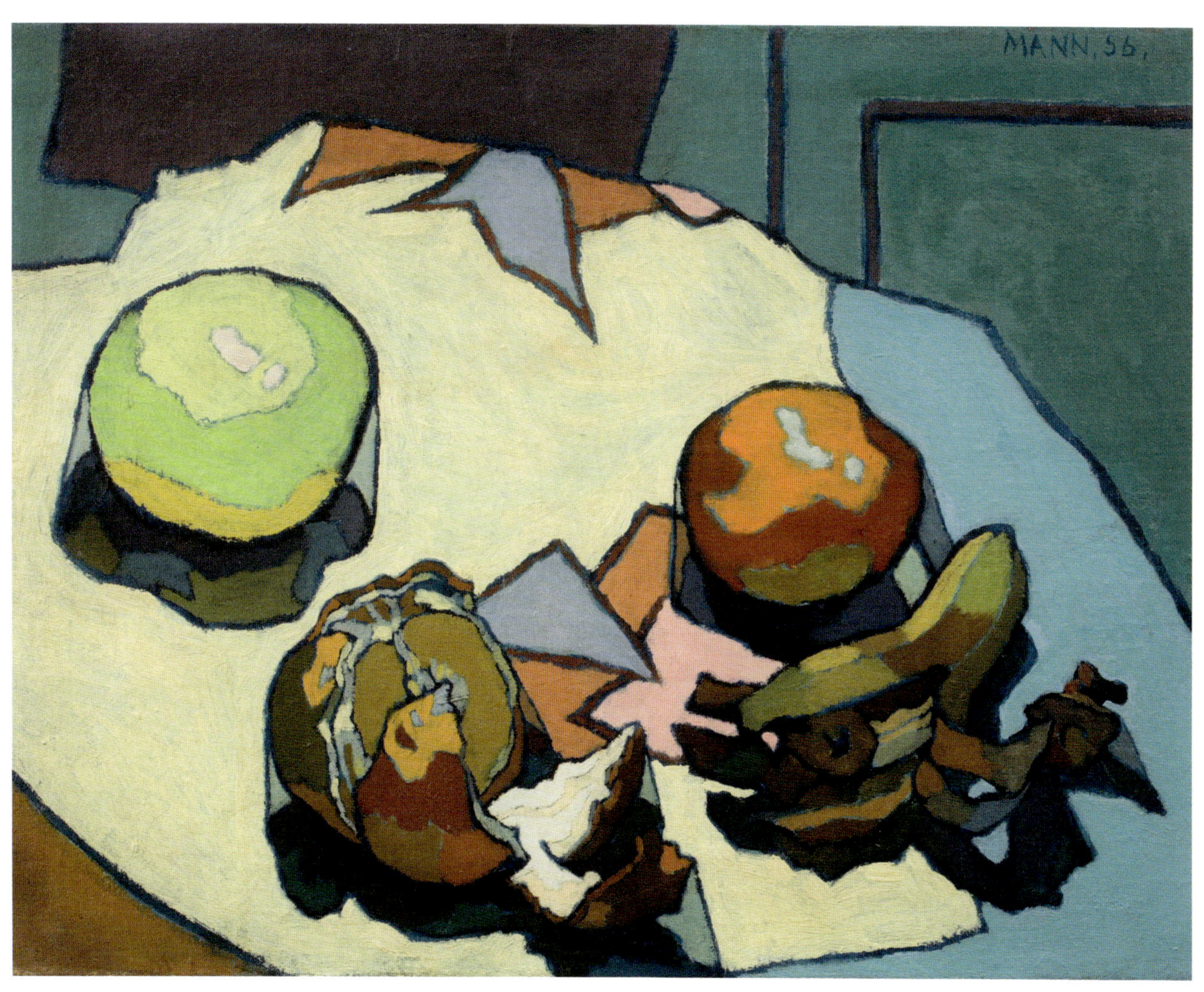
MANN, 56,

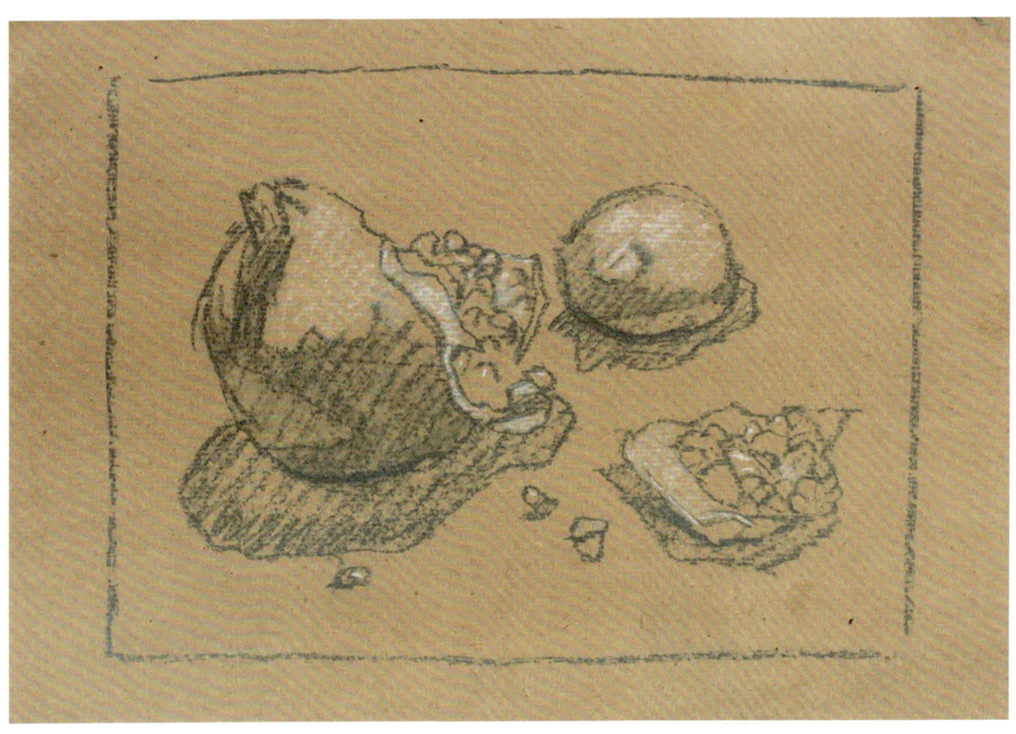

22.

Study for Pomegranate and Lemon, c.1957

Chalk on paper
26 × 40.1 cm / 10¼ × 15¾ in

Provenance
The Artist's Estate

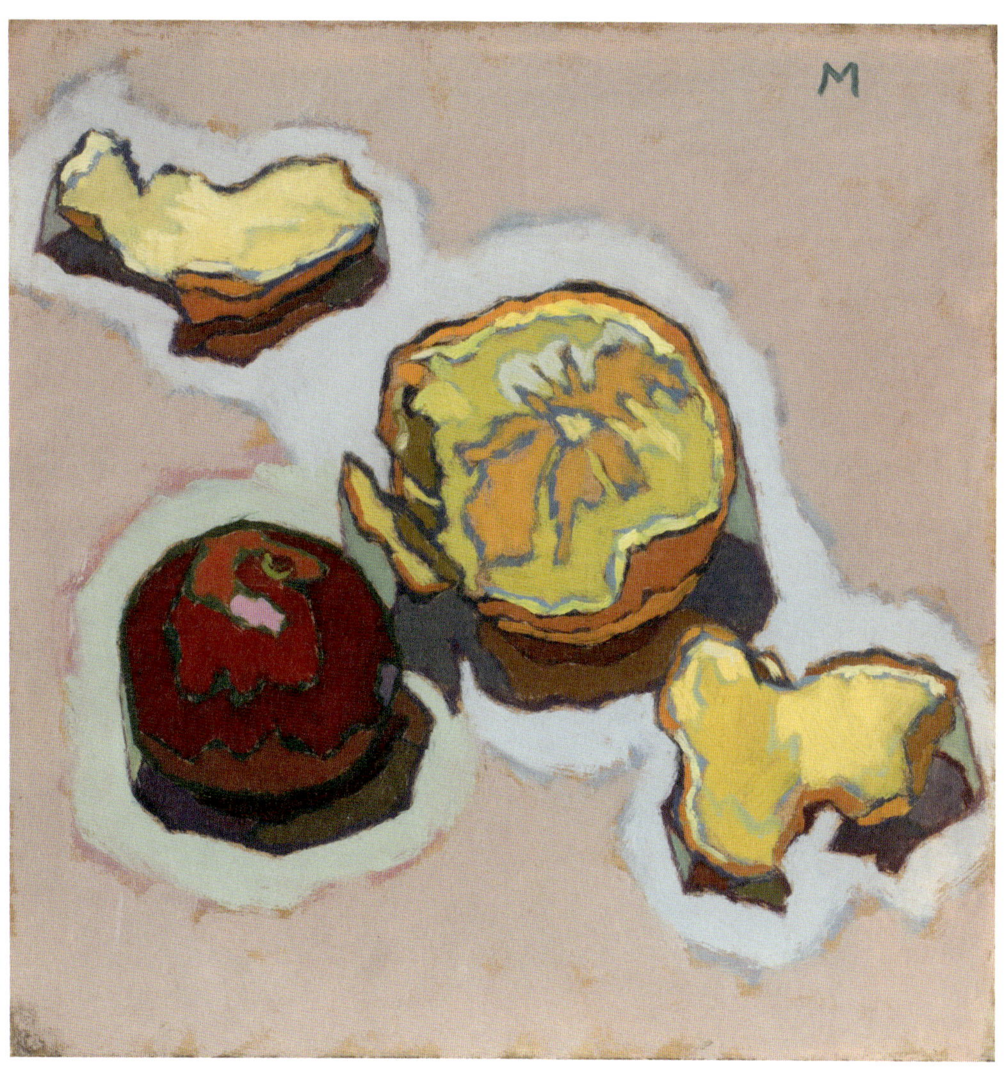

23.

Still Life with Pomegranate, c.1957

Signed upper right 'M'
Oil on board
30 × 30 cm / 11¾ × 11¾ in

Provenance
The Artist's Estate

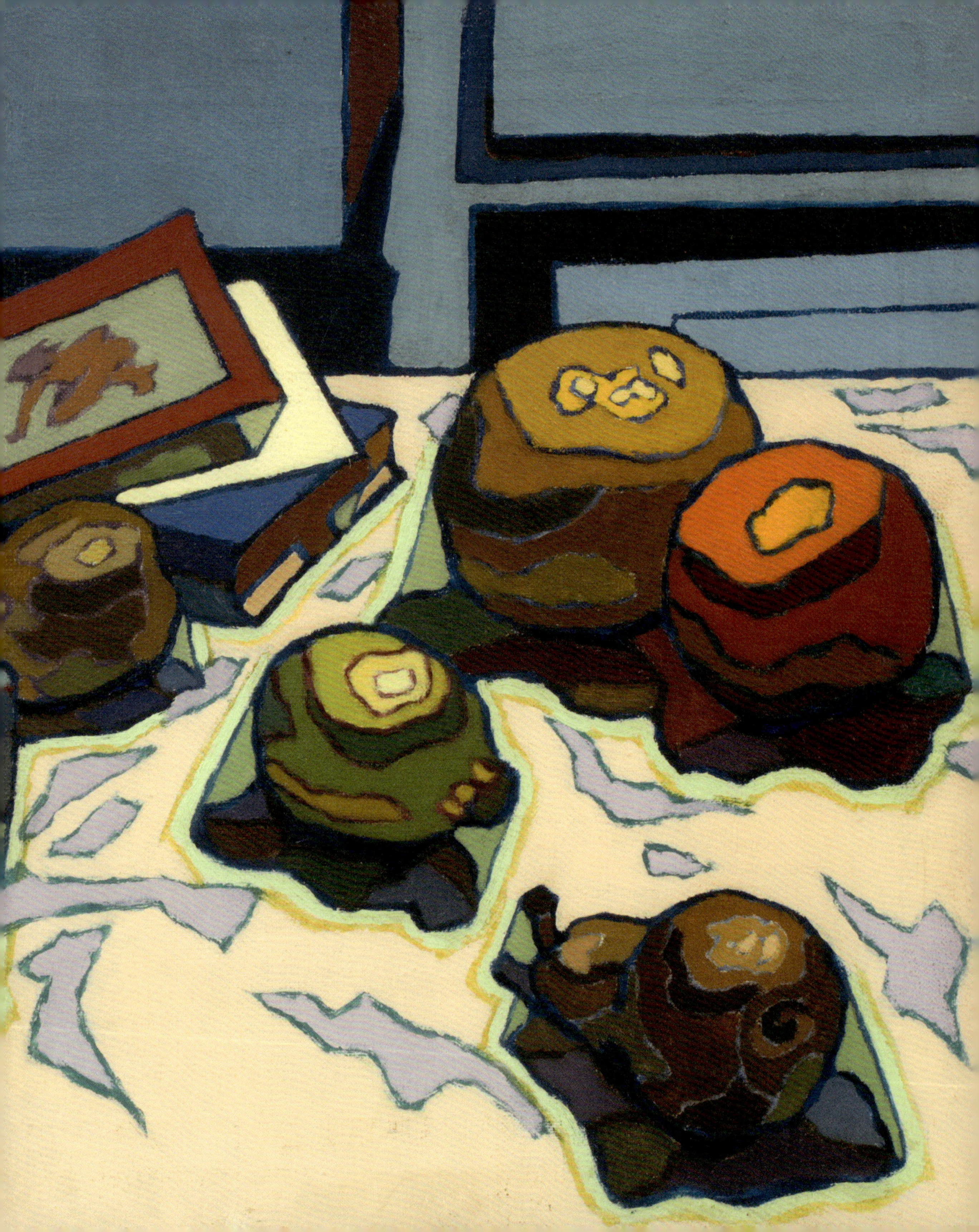

CHRONOLOGY

1911
Cyril Mann was born in Paddington.

1914
Mann's family returned to their native Nottingham at the outbreak of the First World War.

1918
Mann's father returned from the War with shell shock. He was admitted to a mental hospital where he remained until his death. Mann and his siblings were brought up by their mother, Gertrude Nellie Mann.

1923
Mann won a scholarship to Nottingham School of Art. He was just twelve, the youngest of any entrant to win a scholarship to the School.

1927
Mann travelled to Canada and became a missionary.

1928
He soon abandoned his life as a missionary, preferring physical labour in mining and timber. He was inspired by his surroundings on the Canadian border, and he started painting again when he met Arthur Lismer, a member of the Canadian post-impressionist Group of Seven.

1933
Mann returned to England at Lismer's suggestion, settling in London. He started painting watercolours in the Paddington and Maida Vale areas.

1935
Mann was introduced to Erica Marx, a wealthy patron of the arts who provided a trust fund for him to study at the Royal Academy Schools.

1938
Mann left the Royal Academy and moved to Paris where he studied under the Scottish Colourist J.D. Fergusson. (Mann later joked that if he had been Scottish, his reputation would have been secured as one of the Colourists.)

1939
Mann returned to London at the outbreak of the Second World War and married Mary Jervis-Read. Their daughter Sylvia was born shortly after their return.

1940 – 5
Mann served as a gunner in the Royal Artillery.

1946
Mann became a conscientious objector when conscripted after the end of the War. His case was heard by a tribunal. In a letter from the time, he objected to fighting 'Russia and China in a future war, because those two countries are honestly trying to create a better life for their people.'

1947 – 9
Mann served as a lecturer at the LCC Central School of Art.

1948
Mann participated in the exhibition, *Artists of Fame and Promise*, at Wildenstein Gallery.

1950
Mann was appointed as a lecturer at Kingsway Day College and the Sir John Cass College. He specialised in the Technology of Painting. He also separated from his wife at this time.

1950s
Mann's work started to be exhibited in several galleries, in both Nottingham and London. Galleries where his work was exhibited include Park Row Gallery, Nottingham, the Brook Street Gallery, Hanover Gallery, and the East End Academy at the Whitechapel Gallery.

1960
Mann married Renske van Slooten. He gave up teaching at this time to concentrate on his painting, while Renske worked to support them. They lived in Bevin Court, a well-known modernist housing project designed by Berthold Lubetkin.

1964
Mann had a one-man show at St Martin's Gallery in the West End.

1965
Mann was given a solo exhibition at Alwin Gallery in Brook Street, Mayfair. Visitors included the Bishop of Woolwich, Dr John Robinson, and the playwright Arnold Wesker.

1966
Mann moved to Walthamstow.

1967
Mann participated in a two-man exhibition at Alwin Gallery.

1968
Mann had a third exhibition at Alwin Gallery.

1969
Mann moved to Leyton, East London, and started depicting subjects from the area, including Epping Forest.

1970
Mann had various private exhibitions, supported by his patrons, Dr and Mrs M. Leibson.

1978
Mann had an exhibition at Ogle Gallery, Eastbourne. He started suffering several mental health problems at this time.

1979
Mann had several spells in Claybury mental hospital.

1980
Mann died in Whipps Cross Hospital on 7 January, aged 69.

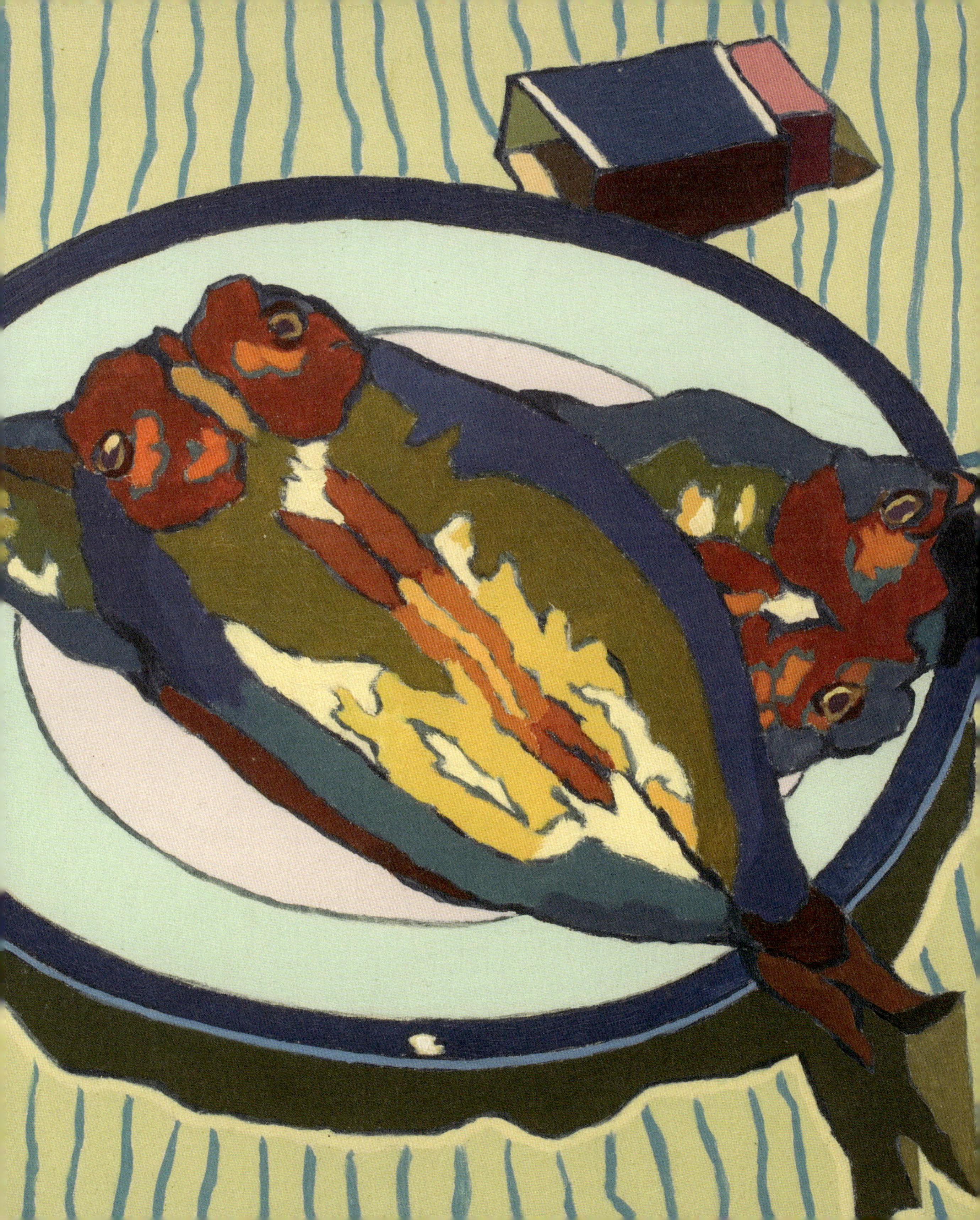

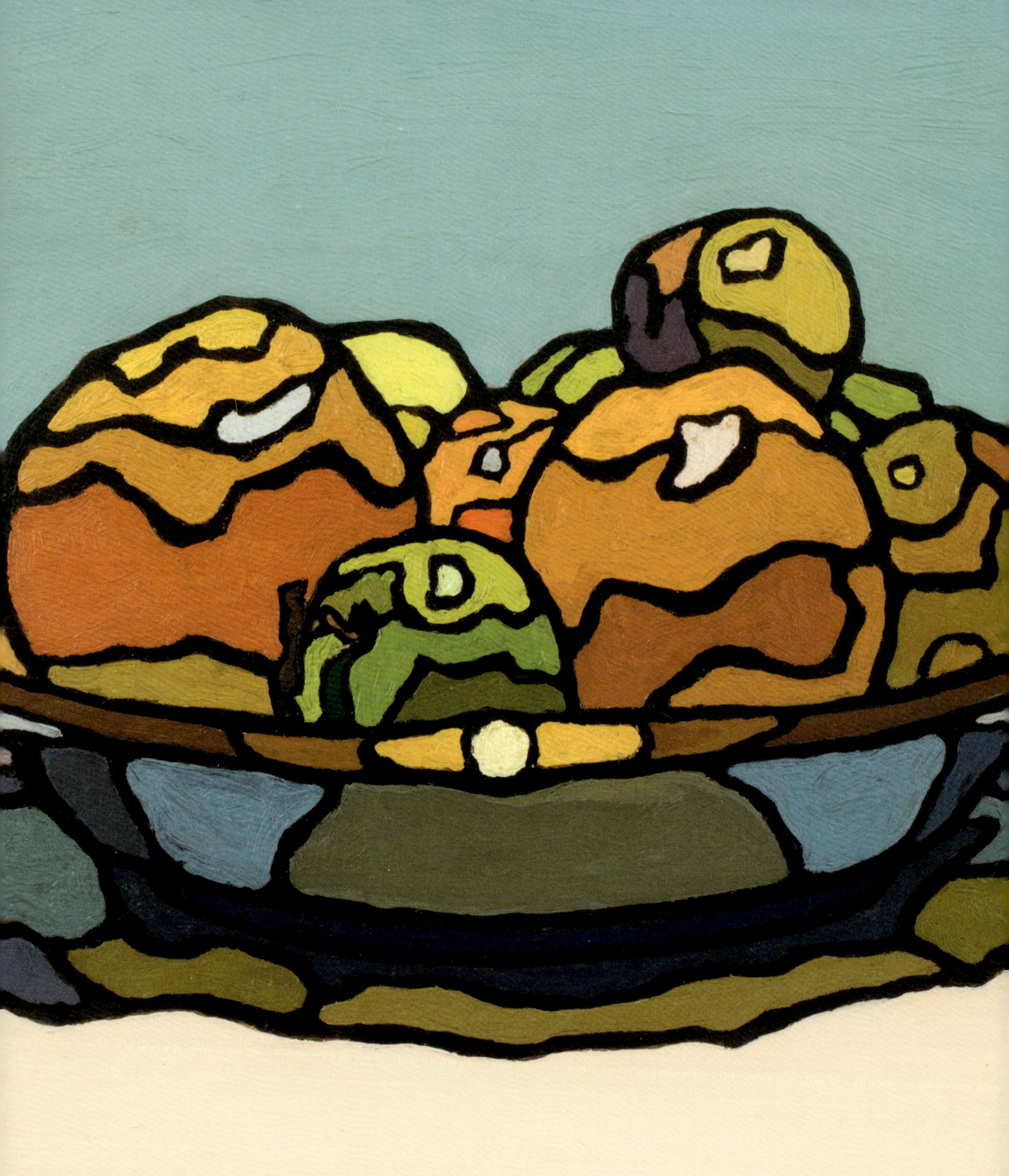

Biography

Cyril Mann was a professional painter that spent much of his life working in obscurity. His work was predominantly in a naturalistic style, distinguished from that of his contemporaries in post-war Britain by an unusually obsessive empiricism. He had talents both as a technician and in matters of compositional rigour, and his enduring achievement is his solid shadow still-life work, produced between 1951 and 1957.

Mann was born in London, though his family was from Nottingham. At the age of three, his family moved back to Nottingham, and when he was just twelve he went to study in the local art school – an impressively young age for such studies. Such early success perhaps enhanced his sense of self-importance as an artist and, later, he demonstrated the anxiety of influence, ignoring the work of his contemporaries and preferring to evoke canonical artists like Vincent Van Gogh and Michelangelo.

After a period in Canada, in which, among other things, he trained as a missionary and worked as a miner, he started painting again in earnest, returning to this career path in 1928. He studied at the Royal Academy Schools between 1935 and 1938 before spending a year in Paris as a pupil of the Scottish colourist, J.D. Fergusson. He returned to London in 1939, when he started making vibrant still-life paintings. He also married Mary Jervis-Read at this time, with whom he had a daughter, though they later divorced in 1950. After the war he depicted many bomb-damaged sites. By the late nineteen-forties his work started to be exhibited at a number of galleries in London, most notably in *Artists of Fame and Promise* at the Wildenstein Gallery in 1948.

To support his painting, Mann also lectured, first at the LCC Central School of Art from 1948, and then at the Kingsway Day College and the Sir John Cass College from 1950. He struggled in poverty for much of his career, though his second wife, Renske van Slooten, brought some financial relief, earning a living to support them both. Mann married her in 1960. He spent the last fifteen years of his life working in East London, first in Walthamstow, then in Leyton. He suffered mental health problems towards the end of his life and died in hospital at the age of sixty-nine. His work is now in the collections of the William Morris Gallery, Walthamstow, the Guildhall Art Gallery, London, and the British Museum.

COLOPHON

First published to accompany the exhibition

Cyril Mann: The Solid Shadow Paintings

Piano Nobile
28 November 2018 - 26 January 2019

Piano Nobile Publications No. XLVIII 2018
ISBN: 978-1-901192-52-0

Editor
Matthew Travers

Text
Luke Farey

Coordination
Annabel Niekirk

Design
Graham Rees Design

Print and Binding
Graphius

Photography
Colin Mills

Acknowledgements

Piano Nobile wishes to express our sincere gratitude to Renske Mann and the estate of Cyril Mann for their assistance in the preparation of this exhibition.

Distributed by Casemate Group
10 Hythe Bridge Street, Oxford, OX1 2EW
casemategroup.com

Piano Nobile specialises in Modern and Contemporary British and International works of art. The gallery also represents a select stable of contemporary artists and artists' estates. Established in 1985, Piano Nobile provides expert advice for individuals, corporations and institutions on appraisals, acquisitions and dispersals. With a discerning curatorial vision, the gallery has established a reputation for authoritative exhibitions and publications under the gallery's imprint, Piano Nobile Publications.

Frontispiece:
Cat. 3, Dahlias in Blue Vase, c.1953

Contents (opposite):
Cat. 9, Still Life with Bottles, c.1956

Fig. 1: Page 6
Cyril Mann (1911 - 1980) Self-Portrait, c.1957, The Artist's Estate

Fig. 2: Page 8
Charles Ginner (1878 – 1952) Victoria Embankment Gardens, 1912, Tate Collection, London, © Tate, London 2018

Fig. 3: Page 9
Cyril Mann (1911 – 1980) Drawing of an Apple with Colour Notes, c.1955, The Artist's Estate

Fig. 4: Page 11
Patrick Caulfield (1936 – 2005) Vases of Flowers, 1962, Tate Collection, London, © Tate, London 2018

Fig. 5: Page 15
John Wesley (b.1928) Queen Victoria at Rest, 1989, Private Collection

Page 50
Cat. 20, Still Life with Mug, c.1956

Page 53
Cat. 19, Mackerel, c.1956

Page 54
Cat. 7, Dish of Fruit, c.1955

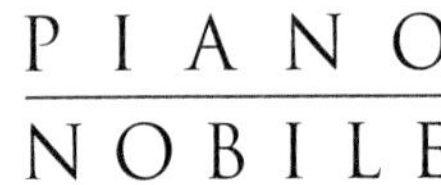

PIANO NOBILE | ROBERT TRAVERS WORKS OF ART LTD
129 Portland Road | London W11 4LW | +44 (0)20 7229 1099
info@piano-nobile.com | piano-nobile.com